I0448442

May 2013

NUCLEAR REACTOR LICENSE RENEWAL

NRC Generally Follows Documented Procedures, but Its Revisions to Environmental Review Guidance Have Not Been Timely

May 2013

NUCLEAR REACTOR LICENSE RENEWAL

NRC Generally Follows Documented Procedures, but Its Revisions to Environmental Review Guidance Have Not Been Timely

Why GAO Did This Study

Many U.S. commercial nuclear power reactors are reaching the end of their initial 40-year operating period. To continue operating, their owners must renew their licenses with NRC, the independent federal agency responsible for licensing and regulating nuclear reactors. NRC evaluates license renewal applications under two parallel reviews for safety and potential environmental impacts. NRC's license renewal process has received increasing public scrutiny due, in part, to the 2011 disaster at Japan's Fukushima Daiichi nuclear plant.

GAO was asked to review NRC's license renewal process for commercial nuclear power reactors. This report examines (1) the scope of the license renewal process, (2) the extent to which NRC updates its safety and environmental review guidance, (3) the extent to which NRC follows its documented license renewal procedures, and (4) knowledgeable stakeholders' views on the strengths and weaknesses in the license renewal process and any suggestions for improvements. GAO reviewed documents; visited two nuclear power plants selected based on characteristics such as having gone through the license renewal process; assessed the consistency of NRC reviews with documented procedures; and interviewed NRC officials and stakeholders from industry and public interest groups. GAO did not evaluate the adequacy or substance of NRC reviews or the quality of the agency's license renewal procedures.

GAO is not making recommendations. NRC neither agreed nor disagreed with GAO's findings.

View GAO-13-493. For more information, contact Frank Rusco at (202) 512-3841 or ruscof@gao.gov.

What GAO Found

The scope of the Nuclear Regulatory Commission's (NRC) license renewal process focuses on managing the effects of aging on a reactor and its associated systems, structures, and components (i.e. safety) and assessing certain potential environmental impacts of extending a reactor's operating-life. As a result, reviews done as part of this process are not required to address as many topics as reviews for initial licensing, which include security and emergency planning.

NRC has regularly updated the safety review guidance it uses in the license renewal process but has not revised most of its environmental review regulations and guidance since they were first issued. NRC has revised its safety review guidance twice—in 2005 and 2010—and has issued interim updates for selected safety issues between those revisions. In contrast, NRC has not revised most of its environmental review regulations and guidance since they were first issued starting in 1996. NRC regulations state the agency's goal is to review its environmental findings every 10 years and update its license renewal regulations and guidance, if necessary. Consistent with this goal, NRC initiated the revision process in 2003. In December 2012, the NRC Commissioners approved draft regulations, but they directed agency staff to make additional changes. As of March 2013, NRC staff were working on these changes. According to NRC officials, reasons for the lengthy revision process include limited staff resources and competing demands on those resources as well as an unusually large number of technical issues needing evaluation. NRC requires applicants and expects agency staff to consider new and significant environmental information in the license renewal process, but its use of regulations and guidance originally issued 17 years ago has created the impression among some that the agency is using outdated information and has caused uncertainty for some license renewal applicants about what guidance will be used to evaluate their application.

NRC generally followed its procedures when reviewing selected safety and environmental elements in eight license renewal applications GAO examined. NRC's safety reviews were generally consistent with the agency's procedures for evaluating both an applicant's identification of components within the scope of the license renewal process and proposed buried piping and tanks inspection and fire protection programs for aging management. NRC's environmental reviews were also generally consistent with agency procedures for evaluating (1) new and significant information for two generic environmental issues; (2) applicants' assessments of two site-specific environmental issues; and (3) applicants' analyses of alternatives for mitigating severe reactor accidents.

Knowledgeable stakeholders interviewed by GAO identified various perceived strengths and weaknesses and potential improvements to the license renewal process. Stakeholders most often identified NRC staff's technical knowledge and the thoroughness of the agency's reviews as perceived strengths of the process. Stakeholders also identified a range of perceived weaknesses in the license renewal process, including claims that its scope is too narrow and that its public hearing process is flawed and inhibits meaningful public participation. Accordingly, some stakeholders suggested potential changes to improve the license renewal process, including broadening the scope of NRC's reviews and modifying aspects of the public hearing process.

_____ **United States Government Accountability Office**

Contents

Abbreviations

ACRS Advisory Committee on Reactor Safeguards
NRC   Nuclear Regulatory Commission
OIG   Office of the Inspector General

May 30, 2013

Congressional Requesters

U.S. commercial nuclear power reactors generated nearly 20 percent of the nation's electricity in 2012, but many of them are reaching or have reached the end of their initial 40-year operating period.[1] For these reactors to continue operating, their owners must renew their licenses with the Nuclear Regulatory Commission (NRC), the independent federal agency responsible for licensing and regulating nuclear reactors and overseeing their safe operation and security. NRC allows reactor owners to apply for renewal of their operating licenses for up to an additional 20 years, and owners may apply to renew licenses more than once. Since 2000, NRC has renewed operating licenses for 73 of the nation's nuclear reactors.[2] As of May 2013, NRC was reviewing license renewal applications for 14 reactors and expected to receive renewal applications for 15 more reactors in the next 5 years, according to NRC documents.[3] With relatively few new nuclear reactors expected to go into operation in the United States this decade, nuclear power's contribution to the nation's energy supply may depend in large part on the number of existing reactors operating under renewed licenses.

In recent years, NRC's license renewal process has received increasing public scrutiny. In 2007, NRC's Office of the Inspector General (OIG) reported that NRC had developed a comprehensive process for reviewing license renewal applications, but agency staff had not consistently reviewed or independently verified applicant-supplied operating

---

[1]In this report, when we use the term power plant, we are referring to an entire site, and nuclear power reactors are the individual units at each site.

[2]In February 2013, the owner of the Crystal River Nuclear Plant in Florida permanently shut down that site's reactor and, in May 2013, the owner of the Kewaunee Power Station in Wisconsin permanently shut down that site's reactor. These actions reduced the number of operating commercial nuclear power reactors in the United States from 104 to 102. The Kewaunee reactor was one of the 73 reactors with an operating license renewed by NRC. As a result, as of May 2013, there are 72 commercial nuclear power reactors with renewed operating licenses operating in the United States.

[3]The owner of the Watts Bar nuclear reactor in Tennessee—whose initial operating license does not expire until 2035—has not submitted a license renewal application and has not notified NRC of its intent to submit an application.

experience information.[4] In 2011, following the disaster at Japan's Fukushima Daiichi nuclear power plant,[5] more than 40 public interest groups and individuals called for a moratorium on license renewal decisions until NRC completed its review of lessons learned from the disaster and issued any regulatory decisions and environmental analyses based on those lessons. In May 2012, NRC held a public meeting to collect comments on issues for the agency to consider as it prepares for future reviews of applications to renew reactor operating licenses for a second time. Renewing an operating license for a second time would allow a reactor to operate for a total of up to 80 years. In August 2012, the NRC Commissioners suspended all pending license renewal decisions until the agency addresses a federal appeals court decision vacating NRC's Waste Confidence Decision and Temporary Storage Rule, which embodies the agency's generic determination on the environmental impacts of continued storage of spent nuclear fuel beyond the licensed life for nuclear reactor operations and prior to its ultimate disposal in a geologic repository.[6] According to agency documents, NRC has historically used this generic determination to satisfy the agency's

---

[4]NRC Office of the Inspector General, *Audit of NRC's License Renewal Program*, OIG-07-A-15 (Washington, D.C.: September 2007).

[5]On March 11, 2011, a 9.0-magnitude earthquake and subsequent tsunami devastated northeast Japan. The Fukushima Daiichi nuclear power plant suffered extensive damage when a tsunami wave that exceeded the plant's seawall flooded the site and caused a prolonged loss of electrical power at several of its reactors. As a result of the loss of power, plant operators were unable to keep three of the reactors cool, which led to fuel melting, hydrogen explosions, and the release of radioactive material into the environment. The disaster displaced tens of thousands of residents and contaminated the surrounding area. The Japanese government expects recovery to take years and cost billions of dollars.

[6]On June 8, 2012, the U.S. Court of Appeals for the District of Columbia Circuit found that some aspects of NRC's 2010 Waste Confidence Decision Update and associated Temporary Storage Rule did not satisfy the agency's National Environmental Policy Act obligations and vacated the Decision Update and Rule. According to a NRC document, the Waste Confidence Decision and Rule represent NRC's generic determination that spent nuclear fuel can be stored safely and without significant environmental impacts for a period of time after the end of the licensed life of a nuclear reactor. See 75 Fed. Reg. 81,037 (Dec. 23, 2010). The court held that NRC needed to examine the potential environmental impacts of failing to secure permanent disposal for spent nuclear fuel, the risk of potential spent fuel pool leaks, and the potential consequences of spent fuel pool fires. In response to the court's decision, NRC decided to stop all final licensing decisions that rely on the Waste Confidence Decision and Rule, including license renewals, but it directed that agency staff should continue all licensing reviews and proceedings. The NRC Commissioners have directed agency staff to issue the final Environmental Impact Statement and Rule to address the court's concerns by no later than September 2014.

obligations under the National Environmental Policy Act[7] with respect to continued spent fuel storage and has incorporated the generic determination by reference into license renewal supplemental environmental impact statements.

In this context, you asked us to review NRC's license renewal process for commercial nuclear power reactors. This report examines (1) the scope of the license renewal process; (2) the extent to which NRC updates the safety and environmental review guidance used in the license renewal process; (3) the extent to which NRC follows the agency's documented license renewal procedures; and (4) knowledgeable stakeholders' views on the strengths and weaknesses in the license renewal process and suggestions, if any, for improving the process.

To conduct this work, we reviewed relevant laws, regulations, and NRC guidance and interviewed NRC headquarters and regional officials involved in the license renewal process. To describe the scope of the license renewal process, we reviewed NRC regulations and guidance. In addition, we visited a nonprobability sample of two nuclear power plants—Millstone Power Station in Connecticut and the Pilgrim Nuclear Power Station in Massachusetts—to interview plant representatives about their experience with the license renewal process and to observe programs implemented at the sites following a license renewal.[8] We selected these sites to capture a variety of characteristics, including sites that had gone through the license renewal process, at least one site that was operating under a renewed license beyond its initial 40-year operating period, and at least one site that was the subject of a public hearing concerning a challenge to its license renewal application. To determine the extent to which NRC updates the safety and environmental review guidance used in the license renewal process, we examined NRC documents, reviewed changes made to license renewal safety and

---

[7]Pub. L. No. 91-190, 83 Stat. 852 (1970), codified as amended at 42 U.S.C. §§ 4321-4347 (2013). Under the National Environmental Policy Act, federal agencies must assess the effects of major federal actions—those they propose to carry out or to permit—that significantly affect the environment. The National Environmental Policy Act has two principal purposes: (1) to ensure that an agency carefully considers detailed information concerning significant environmental impacts and (2) to ensure that this information will be made available to the public.

[8]Because this was a nonprobability sample, the information we gathered from these site visits is not generalizable to all nuclear power plants but provides important illustrative information.

environmental guidance, and interviewed NRC officials. To determine the extent to which NRC followed the agency's documented license renewal procedures, we selected a nonprobability sample of safety and environmental review elements that are assessed as part of NRC's license renewal process and identified the agency's documented procedures for reviewing those elements. We then identified the actions NRC staff took to review the selected elements, as documented in NRC audit reports, inspection reports, and final safety and environmental reports, for a nonprobability sample of eight license renewal applications. Our nonprobability sample consisted of license renewal applications for Columbia Generating Station, Duane Arnold Energy Center, Millstone Power Station (Unit 3), Monticello Nuclear Generating Plant, Pilgrim Nuclear Power Station, Shearon Harris Nuclear Power Plant, Virgil C. Summer Nuclear Station, and Wolf Creek Generating Station.[9] We selected this sample to capture a variety of characteristics, including reactors from different NRC regions, and reactors whose license renewal applications were reviewed using different versions of NRC's safety and environmental review guidance. We then compared NRC staff's documented actions with the agency's documented procedures to assess the level of consistency for the review elements in our sample. We did not evaluate the adequacy or substance of NRC's review actions or the quality of its documented license renewal procedures. To describe knowledgeable stakeholders' views of strengths and weaknesses in NRC's license renewal process, we interviewed 15 stakeholders. To ensure coverage and a range of perspectives, we selected stakeholders who came from industry, public interest groups, state governments, and NRC's Advisory Committee on Reactor Safeguards (ACRS).[10] We analyzed stakeholders' responses to a standard set of questions and

---

[9]Because this was a nonprobability sample, our results are not generalizable to all license renewal reviews but provide examples of safety and environmental review elements that NRC reviewed as part of its license renewal process.

[10]ACRS is a body of nuclear, engineering, and safety experts appointed by the NRC Commissioners, which is independent of the NRC staff and reports directly to the NRC Commissioners. ACRS is established in statute. The committee has four primary purposes: (1) to review and report on safety studies and reactor facility license and license renewal applications; (2) to advise the NRC Commissioners on the hazards of proposed and existing production and utilization facilities and the adequacy of proposed safety standards; (3) to initiate reviews of specific generic matters or nuclear facility safety-related items; and (4) to provide advice in the areas of health physics and radiation protection.

summarized the results. Appendix I presents a more detailed description of our objectives, scope, and methodology.

We conducted this performance audit from May 2012 to May 2013 in accordance with generally accepted government auditing standards. Those standards require that we plan and perform the audit to obtain sufficient, appropriate evidence to provide a reasonable basis for our findings and conclusions based on our audit objectives. We believe that the evidence obtained provides a reasonable basis for our findings and conclusions based on our audit objectives.

Background

NRC issues licenses for commercial nuclear power reactors to operate for up to 40 years and allows these licenses to be renewed for up to an additional 20 years.[11] There is no set limit on the number of times a reactor's operating license can be renewed. Most of the nation's 102 operating commercial nuclear power reactors received their initial operating licenses in the 1970s and 1980s.[12] By the end of 2013, 64 reactors will have held an operating license for at least 30 years, and of these reactors, 20 will have held an operating license for 40 years or more (see fig. 1). As a result, many reactors are reaching or have reached the end of their initial 40-year operating period. As of May 2013, NRC had renewed 73 reactor licenses and was reviewing license renewal applications for 14 reactors.

---

[11]The decision to seek license renewal rests entirely with reactor owners and, according to NRC documents, is typically based on the reactor's economic situation and whether it can meet NRC requirements.

[12]One reactor received its operating license in 1969, and 6 reactors received their operating licenses in the 1990s, with the last of those reactors receiving its operating license in 1996. The other 95 reactors received their operating licenses from 1970 through 1989. Appendix II lists, for each of the nation's operating reactors, the date of their initial operating license, their license renewal status, and the date their current license is set to expire.

Figure 1: Operating Commercial Nuclear Power Reactors and Their License Renewal Status as of May 2013

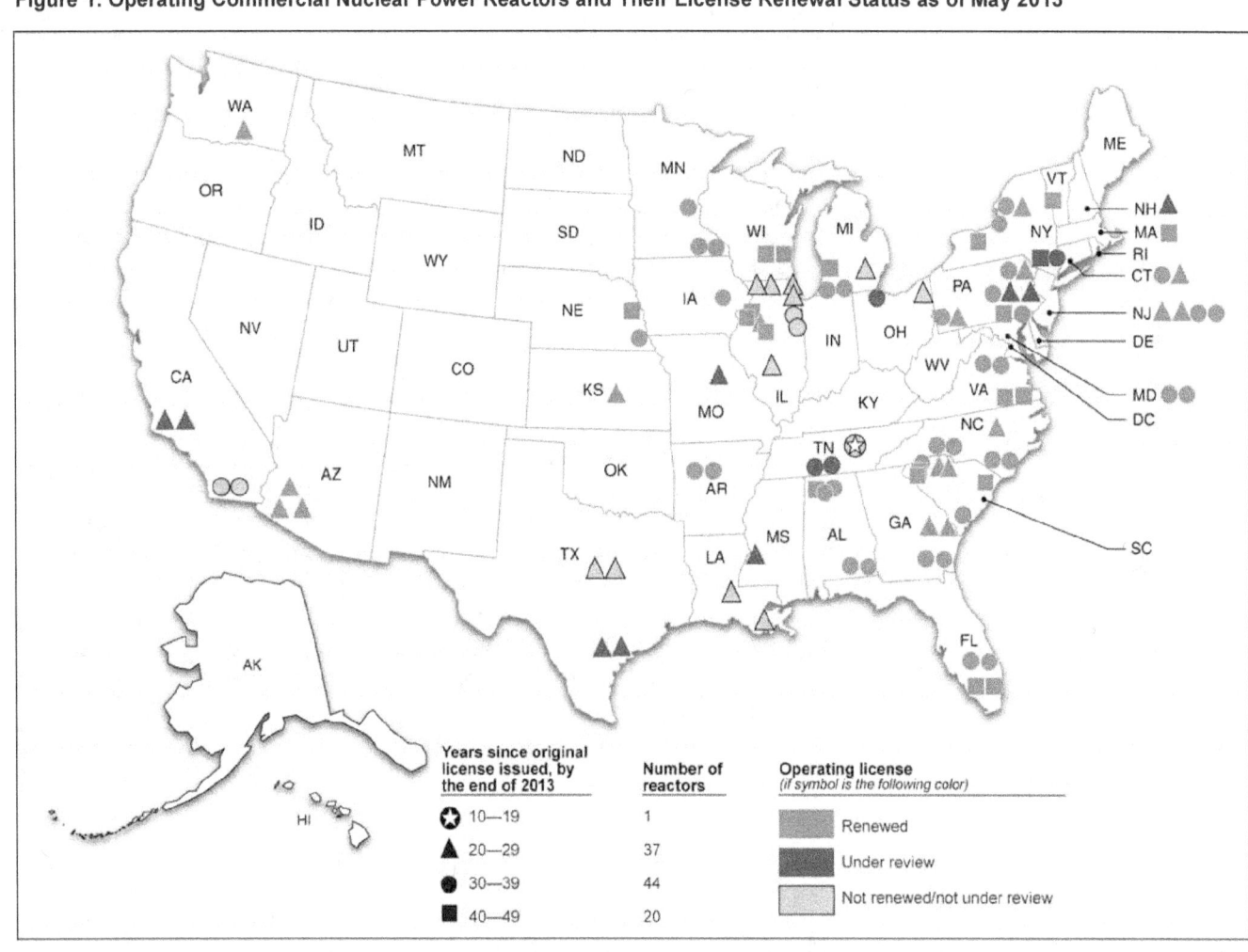

Years since original license issued, by the end of 2013	Number of reactors
⭐ 10—19	1
▲ 20—29	37
● 30—39	44
■ 40—49	20

Operating license *(if symbol is the following color)*

	Renewed
	Under review
	Not renewed/not under review

Sources: NRC (data); Map Resources (map).

Note: In February 2013, the owner of the Crystal River Nuclear Plant in Florida permanently shut down that site's reactor and, in May 2013, the owner of the Kewaunee Power Station in Wisconsin permanently shut down that site's reactor. These actions reduced the number of operating commercial nuclear power reactors in the United States from 104 to 102. The Kewaunee reactor was one of the 73 reactors with an operating license renewed by NRC. As a result, as of May 2013, there are 72 commercial nuclear power reactors with renewed operating licenses operating in the United States.

NRC has used its documented license renewal process for commercial nuclear reactors since the first license renewal application was submitted in 1998. The process begins when a reactor owner submits an application to NRC to renew its operating license (see fig. 2).[13] The application must include two evaluations: (1) a safety review on the aging of certain systems, structures, and components and a description of the programs the applicant plans to use to manage the negative effects of aging during the reactor's extended operating-life and (2) an environmental review on the potential environmental impacts if the reactor operates for another 20 years. NRC staff review the application through audits and by requesting additional information from applicants to address any staff questions.[14] Agency staff also verify through inspections that applicants meet license renewal requirements and have implemented programs and activities consistent with their application and NRC's safety review. The public may submit comments and attend meetings at several points during the license renewal process. In addition, a person whose interest may be affected by the renewal can file a written request for a hearing or a petition for leave to intervene in the renewal of the license, and those challenges may be litigated in a public hearing before NRC's Atomic Safety and Licensing Board if certain requirements are met. ACRS—an independent body of nuclear, engineering, and safety experts appointed by the NRC Commissioners—reviews the NRC staff's final safety report

---

[13]According to NRC regulations, a reactor owner may apply to renew its operating license as early as 20 years before expiration of the current license, 10 C.F.R. § 54.17(c) (2013). There is no limit on how late a reactor owner can apply for license renewal. However, according to NRC regulations, if a reactor owner files a license renewal application that is sufficient for NRC's review at least 5 years before expiration of its existing license, and the agency is reviewing the application at the end of the 5 years, the reactor's operating license will not be deemed to have expired until NRC has reached a final determination on its application, 10 C.F.R. § 2.109(b) (2013). If a sufficient application is not submitted at least 5 years before the current license expires, and the current license expires before the review has been completed, the reactor will have to cease operations unless an exemption to 10 C.F.R. § 2.109(b) is granted.

[14]According to NRC documents, agency staff uses requests for additional information to obtain the information they need to make a regulatory decision that is fully informed, technically correct, and legally defensible. Requests for additional information are necessary when the information was not included in an applicant's initial submission, is not contained in any other docketed correspondence, or cannot reasonably be inferred from the information available to agency staff. For example, according to NRC officials, agency staff use requests for additional information during the environmental review to look for new or updated information on the issues they are reviewing as part of the license renewal process.

and inspection findings and makes a recommendation as to whether or not a license renewal application should be approved.

Figure 2: Key Steps of NRC's License Renewal Process for Nuclear Power Reactors

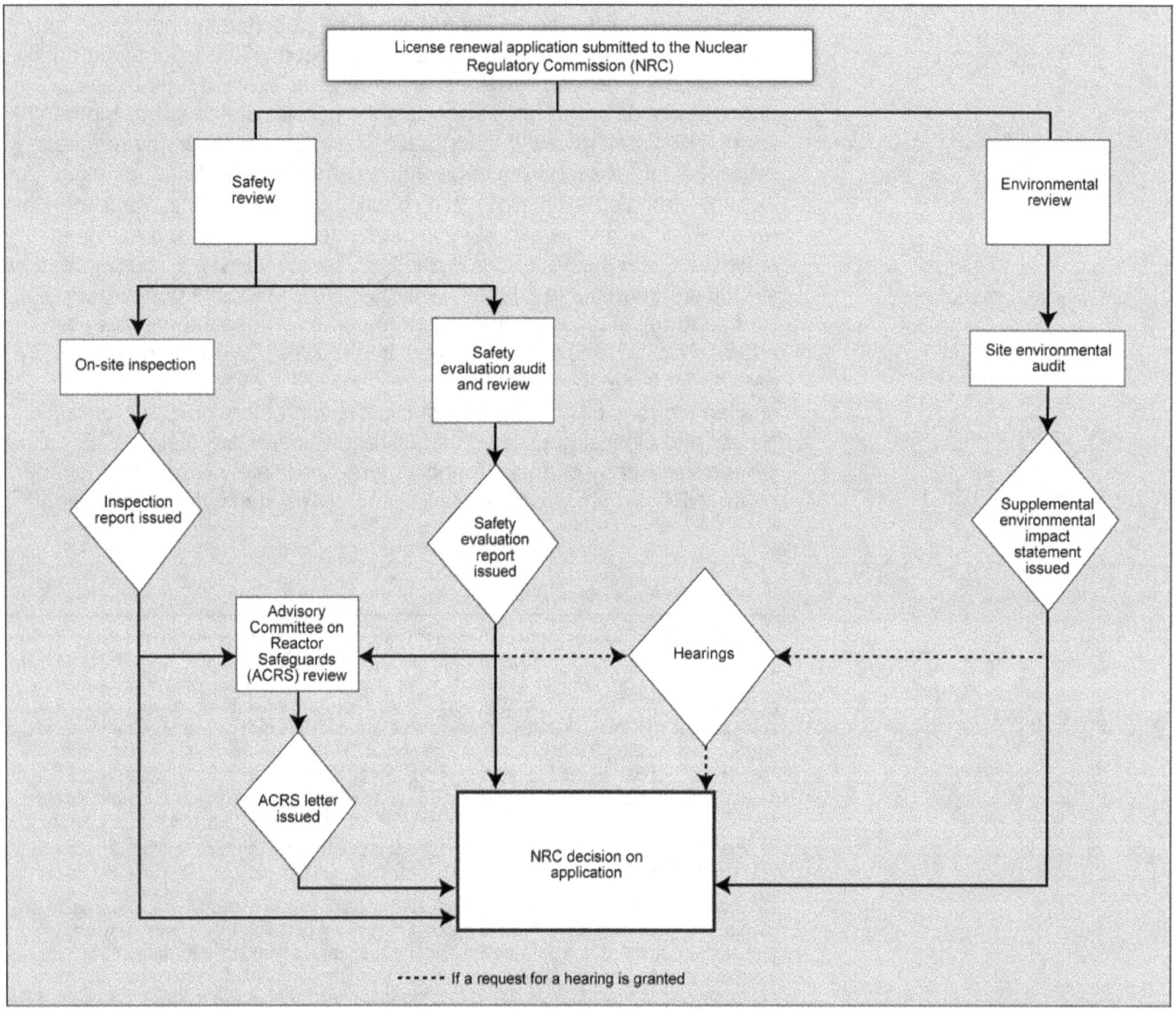

Source: GAO analysis of NRC data.

Once agency staff reviews are finalized, ACRS has made its recommendation, and any Atomic Safety and Licensing Board hearings are completed, NRC makes a final determination on whether or not to renew a reactor's operating license. According to NRC documents, the agency generally expects to complete a license renewal review within 22 months of an application's submission, if there is not a public hearing. If there is a public hearing, the agency generally expects a license renewal review to be completed within 30 months. If NRC renews a reactor's operating license, agency staff perform an additional inspection to verify that the reactor owner has implemented the commitments, license conditions, and aging management programs it agreed to during the license renewal process. The inspection typically happens prior to a reactor operating beyond its initial 40-year operating period.

In September 2007, NRC's OIG issued an audit report detailing its findings on NRC's license renewal safety reviews.[15] Overall, the OIG found that NRC had developed a comprehensive license renewal process but identified eight recommendations for improvement. In particular, the OIG recommended that NRC establish report-writing standards for agency staff describing the license renewal review methodology and supporting the conclusions in license renewal reports. The OIG also recommended that the agency establish requirements and management controls to standardize the depth and conduct of license renewal reviews of plant-specific operating experience. According to the OIG report, reviews of plant-specific operating experience are important for license renewal decisions because they can help identify lessons learned for detecting and monitoring the negative effects of aging on components, as well as appropriate actions that may be taken to address these issues. NRC staff agreed to implement both of these recommendations along with five of the OIG's other recommendations and took steps to implement them.[16] In 2010, the OIG determined that NRC had adequately addressed each recommendation it had agreed to implement. We reviewed NRC reports for license renewal applications that were audited and approved for license renewal after the agency put revised guidance into effect in 2009 to address the OIG's recommendation on standardizing

---

[15]OIG-07-A-15.

[16]The OIG's eighth recommendation was directed to the NRC Commissioners. According to NRC documents, the OIG closed this recommendation in 2008.

the depth and conduct of plant-specific operating experience reviews.[17] We determined the NRC reports documented that agency staff generally followed the revised guidance during on-site audits for those license renewal applications.[18]

Scope of NRC's License Renewal Process Focuses on Managing Aging and Assessing Potential Environmental Impacts

The scope of NRC's license renewal process focuses on managing the negative effects of aging on the reactor and its associated systems, structures, and components, as well as assessing the potential environmental impacts of extending a reactor's operating-life. This scope is reflected in the two reviews that comprise NRC's license renewal process. NRC evaluates license renewal applications through two parallel staff reviews—one focused on safety issues and one focused on the potential environmental impacts of extending a reactor's operating life.[19] NRC has focused the license renewal safety review primarily on whether the applicant has proposed programs that will adequately manage the negative effects of aging on certain nonmoving, long-lived parts, such as piping, structural supports, and cables.[20] NRC includes three categories

---

[17]Specifically, we assessed whether NRC audit and safety evaluation reports documented that agency staff followed NRC's revised guidance during onsite license renewal audits to (1) independently search applicant records for potential operating experience issues, (2) examine the results of this search to find issues concerning aging degradation, and (3) determine whether the applicant appropriately considered these issues in its license renewal application. We reviewed NRC reports for the seven license renewal applications that were audited and approved for license renewal after NRC put its revised guidance into effect in April 2009: Columbia Generating Station, Cooper Nuclear Station, Duane Arnold Energy Center, Hope Creek Generating Station, Kewaunee Power Station, Palo Verde Nuclear Generating Station, and Salem Nuclear Generation Station.

[18]We did not evaluate the adequacy or the substance of NRC staff reviews or the quality of the agency's procedures.

[19]NRC requirements for license renewal, including requirements related to safety, are codified in 10 C.F.R. pt. 54. NRC first promulgated these requirements in 1991. Based on lessons learned from a demonstration program, NRC amended the requirements in 1995. In particular, the agency clarified the requirements to focus on managing the negative effects of aging. NRC environmental review procedures, applicable to license renewal among other things, are codified in 10 C.F.R. pt. 51, along with the agency's regulations for implementing the National Environmental Policy Act. NRC amended these regulations in 1996 to establish requirements specific to the license renewal stage, including the agency's findings on the potential environmental impacts of license renewal.

[20]Nonmoving parts are passive structures and components that perform their intended functions without moving parts or without a change in configuration or properties, such as piping, structural supports, and cables. Long-lived parts are those structures and components that are not subject to replacement based on a qualified life or specified time period, as set forth in 10 C.F.R. § 54.21 (a)(1)(ii).

of systems, structures, and components within the scope of the license renewal process: (1) those that are safety-related; (2) those that are not safety-related, but whose failure could affect safety-related functions; and (3) those that are relied on in safety analyses or plant evaluations to perform a function that demonstrates compliance with specific NRC regulations. Similarly, NRC has focused its license renewal environmental review on assessing a defined set of potential environmental impacts of license renewal. Specifically, a number of issues are evaluated generically for all reactors, rather than separately in each reactor's application. Other issues are evaluated through site-specific reviews of the environmental impacts of license renewal and, according to NRC documents, follow the agency's National Environmental Policy Act regulations.[21]

Because license renewal reviews are not as broad as the reviews NRC conducts during a reactor's initial licensing, a number of topics, such as security and emergency planning, are not considered during the license renewal process.[22] According to NRC documents, the scope of the license renewal process is based on two key principles: (1) that the agency's ongoing regulatory processes are adequate to ensure that all currently operating reactors are operated safely within their licensing bases now and will continue to be in the future, with the possible exception of the negative effects of aging on certain passive, long-lived components; and (2) that, in addition to requirements for aging management, the manner in which these reactors are currently maintained will be similarly maintained beyond the original 40-year operating period. As a result, according to agency documents, NRC has determined that it does not need to evaluate license renewal applications against the full range of safety requirements considered during a reactor's initial licensing. Instead, it can focus its review on how the negative effects of aging on certain components will be managed in the years after a reactor's original 40-year operating period.[23] For example, risks of

---

[21]10 C.F.R. pt. 51 (2013).

[22]According to NRC officials, safety-related concerns that fall outside the scope of the license renewal process are to be addressed under other NRC regulations, which apply on an ongoing basis, including during the license renewal period.

[23]NRC, *Foundation for the Adequacy of the Licensing Bases: A Supplement to the Statement of Considerations for the Rule on Nuclear Power Plant License Renewal (10 C.F.R. Part 54),* NUREG-1412 (Washington, D.C.: 1991).

seismic events such as earthquakes are not explicitly covered in the license renewal safety review because NRC considers these to be ongoing safety matters that are addressed at all reactors. According to NRC documents, if new seismic information was identified, NRC would act on that information through its ongoing regulatory processes, regardless of whether a reactor had received a renewed operating license or not. For example, after it was determined that the potential risk posed by earthquake hazards for some nuclear power reactors in the central and eastern United States might be larger than previously estimated, NRC initiated a program to examine the implications of the new seismic hazard estimates for reactors operating in those regions of the country.[24]

NRC Has Regularly Updated Its Safety Review Guidance but Has Not Revised Most of Its Environmental Review Guidance

NRC has regularly updated its safety review guidance for the license renewal process by formally revising key documents on a periodic basis and by issuing interim staff guidance on selected safety issues between revisions, but it has not revised most of the environmental review regulations and guidance since their original issuance. In 2001, the agency issued its original safety review guidance, including a standard review plan for each element of the safety review[25] and a technical report that documents the staff's generic evaluation of aging management programs and provides the technical basis for determining whether applicant programs are adequate for the extended period of operation authorized by a renewed license.[26] NRC has revised these guidance documents twice—in 2005 and 2010—to reflect lessons learned during previous license renewal reviews and new operating experience information. Additionally, NRC has issued interim updates to its safety

---

[24]NRC, *Implications of Updated Probabilistic Seismic Hazard Estimates in Central and Eastern United States,* Generic Issue 199 (Washington, D.C.: June 9, 2005).

[25]NRC, *Standard Review Plan for Review of License Renewal Applications for Nuclear Power Plants,* NUREG-1800 (Washington, D.C.: July 2001).

[26]NRC, *Generic Aging Lessons Learned (GALL) Report,* NUREG-1801 (Washington, D.C.: July 2001).

review guidance for selected safety issues between formal revisions.[27] For example, since the last revision of the safety review guidance in 2010, NRC has issued four final interim guidance documents that have updated the agency's guidance on such topics as an acceptable approach for managing the negative effects of aging on buried and underground piping and tanks.[28] Interim guidance updates are then integrated into the safety review guidance during the next formal revision. According to NRC officials, the agency does not wait for guidance updates to be finalized to address new issues; NRC staff are expected to address such issues as they are identified for applications currently under review and future applications, typically through requests for additional information.

In contrast, NRC has not revised most of the environmental review regulations and guidance for the license renewal process since those documents were first issued starting 17 years ago.[29] In 1996, in anticipation of the first license renewal applications, NRC published a generic environmental impact statement that examined the potential

---

[27]NRC's license renewal interim staff guidance process allows agency staff, industry, and stakeholders to propose changes to certain license renewal guidance documents. According to NRC documents, the process is meant to capture and communicate new insights, lessons learned, and emergent issues with each renewed license. NRC staff are expected to evaluate proposed guidance changes, develop draft interim staff guidance, issue the draft interim staff guidance for public comment, evaluate any comments received, and, if necessary, issue final interim staff guidance. Once approved, the final interim staff guidance supersedes prior guidance and is incorporated by NRC staff into a formal license renewal guidance document revision. NRC expects agency staff to follow the new guidance when reviewing license renewal applications and expects current and future applicants to address the new guidance in the license renewal process. Reactor owners with previously-renewed licenses may voluntarily use interim staff guidance. The interim staff guidance process applies to both the license renewal safety review guidance and portions of the environmental review guidance.

[28]According to NRC officials, almost all interim guidance issued for the license renewal process has been updates to the safety review guidance and not the environmental review guidance because new information develops at a faster rate for safety issues than for environmental issues. In addition, NRC officials told us they believe the agency's license renewal environmental review is a continuous learning process that uses staff evaluations of applicant-provided information, information in agency guidance, and the staff's independent review to probe more deeply into environmental issues. In the officials' view, this process results in continuous improvement in license renewal environmental reviews such that the use of interim staff guidance for environmental issues would be redundant.

[29]NRC amended its environmental review regulations and guidance in 1999, expanding the agency's generic findings about the environmental impacts resulting from the transportation of fuel and waste to and from a single nuclear power plant.

environmental impacts of renewing reactor operating licenses.[30] In the generic environmental impact statement, NRC identified the 92 potential environmental issues it considered relevant to license renewal. The agency analyzed those potential issues and determined which ones it believed could be treated generically in applicant environmental reports and NRC environmental reviews and which ones would require additional site-specific analysis by both applicants and NRC.[31] Later that same year, NRC promulgated regulations that incorporated the findings from its generic environmental impact statement and defined the number and scope of environmental issues that applicants and NRC would have to address during license renewal reviews.[32] Based on these 1996

---

[30]NRC, *Generic Environmental Impact Statement for License Renewal of Nuclear Plants: Main Report*, NUREG-1437, Volume 1 (Washington, D.C.: May 1996). The generic environmental impact statement is the technical basis for the environmental issues and findings codified in Appendix B to Subpart A of 10 C.F.R. pt. 51. NRC's license renewal interim staff guidance process does not apply to NRC's generic environmental impact statement findings incorporated into the regulation, as regulations can only be changed through the federal rulemaking process.

[31]Of the 92 potential environmental issues that NRC identified as relevant to license renewal, the agency determined that 69 issues could be treated generically in applicant environmental reports and NRC environmental reviews without additional site-specific analysis unless agency staff found new and significant information on those issues as part of license renewal reviews. NRC categorized potential environmental issues as generic, or category 1, issues if the agency found the issues met three criteria: (1) the environmental impacts associated with the issue applied to either all reactors or, for some issues, to reactors having a specific type of cooling system or other specified reactor or site characteristics; (2) a single significance level (small, moderate, or large) had been assigned to the impacts, except for collective off-site radiological impacts from the fuel cycle and from high-level waste and spent fuel disposal; and (3) NRC analyzed the mitigation of the adverse impacts associated with the issue and determined that additional site-specific mitigation measures were unlikely to be sufficiently beneficial to warrant implementation. NRC further provided that the generic analysis of the issue may be adopted in a site-specific review and associated supplemental environmental impact statement, such that NRC could elect to conduct a site-specific review of the issue if warranted. NRC determined that the remaining 23 potential environmental issues relevant to license renewal did not meet all three criteria and would require additional site-specific analysis. The agency categorized 21 of these potential environmental issues as category 2 issues and left the remaining two issues—environmental justice and chronic effects of electromagnetic fields—uncategorized.

[32]NRC, *Environmental Review for Renewal of Nuclear Power Plant Operating Licenses*, 61 Fed. Reg. 28,467 (June 5, 1996), codified at 10 C.F.R. pt. 51, subpt. A, app. B.

documents,[33] in 1999, NRC issued a standard review plan for agency staff to use in conducting environmental reviews[34] and, in 2000, a guide for applicants outlining the information to include in their license renewal environmental reports.[35]

In its 1996 regulations, NRC established the goal of reviewing its generic environmental impact statement findings every 10 years and updating its environmental review regulations and guidance, if necessary.[36] NRC further stated in an explanatory statement published with the regulations that it intended to begin reviews about 7 years after the latest version of the regulations was issued.[37] Consistent with this intent, in 2003, NRC initiated the process to update its generic environmental impact report, the first step to determine if revisions would be needed to the license renewal environmental review regulations and guidance.[38] However, according to NRC documents, after soliciting public comments on the rulemaking, the agency put the revision process on hold for 2 years due to limited staff resources and competing demands on those resources. Specifically, NRC officials told us the agency postponed the revision process because it decided that completing the large number of licensing actions under consideration at that time—including 16 license renewal reviews—was a higher priority than updating the license renewal

---

[33]NRC promulgated amendments to the regulations in 1996 (clarifying changes and corrections),1997 (minor corrections), 1999 (expanding the generic findings about the environmental impacts due to transportation of fuel and waste to and from a single nuclear power plant), and 2001 (minor correction).

[34]NRC, *Standard Review Plan for Environmental Reviews for Nuclear Power Plants– Supplement 1: Operating License Renewal*, NUREG-1555, Supplement 1 (Washington, D.C.: October 1999).

[35]NRC, *Preparation of Supplemental Environmental Reports for Applications to Renew Nuclear Power Plant Operating Licenses*, Supplement 1 to Regulatory Guide 4.2 (Washington, D.C.: September 2000).

[36]61 Fed. Reg. at 28,468.

[37]61 Fed. Reg. at 28,468.

[38]NRC, *Notice of Intent To Prepare an Environmental Impact Statement for the License Renewal of Nuclear Power Plants and To Conduct Scoping Process*, 68 Fed. Reg. 33,209 (June 3, 2003).

environmental review regulations.[39] NRC restarted the revision process in 2005.[40]

Four years later, in 2009, the agency published proposed revisions for its license renewal environmental review regulations.[41] According to NRC officials, it took the agency 4 years to prepare the proposed revisions due to the unusually large number of technical issues that needed review as part of the rulemaking process, the large number of industry and public comments, the number of guidance documents that needed to be updated, and competing demands on staff resources from additional license renewal reviews. From 2010 to 2012, after re-evaluation based on public comment and other factors, NRC staff made further changes to the language in the proposed regulations and made related changes to its environmental review guidance. In April 2012, NRC staff submitted proposed revisions in a rulemaking package to the NRC Commissioners for approval.[42]

The April 2012 proposed revisions would redefine the number and scope of environmental issues the agency must address during its environmental reviews based on lessons learned and knowledge gained

[39]According to NRC officials, license renewal reviews were priority work because of the importance of maintaining a stable and predictable regulatory process for reactor owners seeking timely review and processing of their license renewal applications.

[40]NRC, *Notice of Extension of the Public Comment Period for Scoping Process To Prepare an Environmental Impact Statement for the License Renewal of Nuclear Power Plants*, 70 Fed. Reg. 57,628 (Oct. 3, 2005).

[41]NRC, Proposed Rule, *Revisions to Environmental Review for Renewal of Nuclear Power Plant Operating Licenses*, 74 Fed. Reg. 38,117 (July 31, 2009). Concurrent with publication of the proposed rule revisions, NRC published for comment the draft revised generic environmental impact statement and proposed revisions to associated guidance (*Regulatory Guide 4.2, Supplement 1, Preparation of Environmental Reports for Nuclear Power Plant License Renewal Applications*, and *Environmental Standard Review Plan, Standard Review Plans for Environmental Reviews for Nuclear Power Plants, Supplement 1: Operating License Renewal*).

[42]Also, in conjunction with a January 2012 briefing to the NRC Commissioners, NRC staff publicly released a "preliminary draft final" revision to the environmental review regulations pertaining to license renewals but did not accept public comment.

from previous license renewal reviews.[43] Among other things, the revisions would

- consolidate related environmental issues that were considered separately in the 1996 environmental review regulations and guidance;
- add several new environmental issues that would be treated generically in applicant environmental reports and NRC environmental reviews, such as the effects of dredging on water quality and the exposure of aquatic and terrestrial organisms to radionuclides; and
- add two new environmental issues that would require site-specific analysis—(1) the potential impact on groundwater quality from the inadvertent discharge of radionuclides into groundwater from reactor systems, piping, and tanks and (2) the cumulative impacts of continued reactor operations during a reactor's extended operating-life.

In addition, according to NRC documents, the agency has committed to developing site-specific analyses for each license renewal review of the potential cumulative impacts of greenhouse gas emissions and global climate change during a reactor's extended operating-life.[44]

In December 2012, the NRC Commissioners approved the rule revisions but directed agency staff to make additional changes, including removing

---

[43]Based on the April 2012 proposed rule revision, NRC would not eliminate any of the 92 environmental issues established in the 1996 environmental review regulations and guidance but would consolidate and group some issues together based on similarities. As a result, the revisions would address 78 environmental issues, 60 of which would be treated generically in applicant environmental reports and NRC environmental reviews, 17 of which would require site-specific analysis, and 1 which would remain uncategorized and not require site-specific analysis.

[44]According to an NRC document, starting in 2008, NRC began to evaluate the effects of greenhouse gas emissions and its implications for global climate change in its site-specific environmental reviews for license renewal applications. In 2009, the NRC Commissioners directed agency staff to consider carbon dioxide and other greenhouse gas emissions in their environmental reviews for licensing actions. NRC included an analysis of greenhouse gas impacts in the final revised generic environmental impact statement but did not include this issue in its April 2012 revisions to the regulations. NRC will not require license renewal applicants to provide information pertaining to greenhouse gas emissions and climate change in their environmental reports, according to a NRC document, except as needed in cumulative impact assessments. However, NRC staff will be directed to develop a site-specific analysis for each license renewal review of the impacts caused by greenhouse gas emissions and climate change related to extending a reactor's operating-life.

references to the NRC Waste Confidence Decision Update and Rule. The Waste Confidence Decision Update and Rule considers the storage of spent fuel after a reactor ceases operation, and it was vacated by the U.S. Court of Appeals in June 2012. According to NRC officials, as of March 2013, agency staff were making these changes and planned to submit a final package of revisions to the NRC Commissioners and then to the *Federal Register* in May 2013.[45] Until the rule revisions are finalized, however, the original versions of NRC's license renewal environmental review regulations and guidance in large part remain in effect.

While the agency's environmental reviews continue to follow regulations issued mostly in 1996 and guidance issued based on those regulations, NRC staff are expected to apply and document the lessons learned and knowledge gained from previous license renewal environmental reviews as part of the agency's ongoing environmental reviews, according to NRC officials.[46] NRC requires reactor owners to include in their applications any new and significant information of which the owner is aware concerning the potential environmental impacts of renewing their license. In addition, NRC procedures direct agency staff to look for new and significant information about environmental issues and to consider this

---

[45]Per the April 2012 rule revisions as approved by the NRC Commissioners, the finalized regulations would go into effect 30 days after they are published in the *Federal Register*, and license renewal applicants who submit license renewal applications a year or more after the publication date would be required to comply with the updated regulations.

[46]According to NRC officials, this includes agency staff addressing and documenting new issues, as appropriate, through NRC's environmental reviews and corresponding requests for additional information, whether or not the issues have been incorporated into the license renewal environmental review regulations and guidance.

information in reviewing license renewal applications.[47] According to NRC documents, the agency considers information to be new and significant if (1) it involves a significant environmental issue that was not covered in the agency's generic environmental impact statement or (2) the information was not considered in that document's analysis and it leads to an impact finding that is different from the finding in the generic environmental impact statement.[48] As of March 2013, according to NRC officials, the agency has never identified information during its license renewal environmental reviews that it considers both new and significant using this definition.[49] During our review of NRC review records for selected license renewal applications, we confirmed that NRC's final supplemental environmental impact statements documented actions agency staff had taken to consider whether, according to NRC's definition, there was new and significant information on environmental issues.[50] The final reports we reviewed indicated that agency staff had considered whether new information existed but determined that none of

---

[47]According to NRC guidance, agency staff are expected to determine if there is new information on environmental issues as part of each license renewal environmental review. If the staff's search identifies new information on an environmental issue, then they are expected to evaluate the information to determine if it is also "significant" under NRC's definition. If agency staff deem the new information to be significant, then additional steps are required to evaluate the information. If agency staff deem the new information to not be significant, then they do not analyze the information further in the supplemental environmental impact statement associated with the license renewal application under review. In this situation, NRC staff are expected to include a section in the supplemental environmental impact statement that (1) describes the search for new information on the specific environmental issue, (2) summarizes any new information the staff identified, (3) presents the staff's evaluation of the significance of the information, and (4) adopts the conclusions in NRC's generic environmental impact statement for that issue.

[48]NRC designates the significance of potential environmental impacts as small, moderate, or large. The agency designates the significance of a potential environmental impact as small if its environmental effects are not detectable or are so minor that they will neither destabilize nor noticeably alter any important attribute of the resource. NRC designates the significance of a potential environmental impact as moderate if its environmental effects are sufficient to alter noticeably, but not to destabilize, important attributes of the resource. The agency designates the significance of a potential environmental impact as large if its environmental effects are clearly noticeable and are sufficient to destabilize important attributes of the resource.

[49]According to NRC officials, agency staff have identified some information they considered "new" but not "significant," such as the issue of radionuclides in groundwater.

[50]We did not evaluate the adequacy or the substance of NRC staff actions.

the information they considered was both new and significant under NRC's definition.

According to NRC's principles of good regulation, regulations should be based on the best available knowledge from research and operational experience, and the agency's strategic plan states that regulatory guidance should be kept up-to-date. Because NRC has not finalized the updates to its license renewal environmental review regulations and guidance, however, the agency's environmental reviews for the 73 license renewals approved to date were made under the regulations originally issued in 1996, as amended and supplemented in 1999, and guidance issued based on those regulations. NRC officials told us that agency staff are to consider and document new information on environmental issues as part of each license renewal environmental review. However, the agency's use of regulations originally issued in 1996 and guidance based on those regulations has created the impression, among some, that NRC is relying on outdated environmental information. For example, several representatives of public interest groups told us they believe NRC's delay in revising its environmental review regulations and guidance means the agency is using outdated information in its license renewal reviews. In addition, according to NRC's principles of good regulation, regulations, once established, should be perceived to be reliable. The prolonged presence of draft revisions to NRC's environmental review regulations and guidance alongside current regulations and guidance can create uncertainty for license renewal applicants. For example, some industry representatives we interviewed said NRC's delay in finalizing the revisions after proposed revisions were published in 2009 had created some uncertainty about what information reactor owners would have to provide and which version of the guidance they would be held to by NRC staff during their environmental review.

NRC Generally Followed Documented Procedures When Evaluating the License Renewal Application Elements We Reviewed

NRC generally followed its documented procedures when reviewing selected safety and environmental elements in the eight license renewal applications we reviewed.[51] Specifically, we reviewed whether NRC reports documented that agency staff had followed NRC's procedures; we did not evaluate the adequacy or the substance of NRC's reviews or the quality of its procedures. We found that NRC's reviews of the following safety elements were generally consistent with the agency's documented procedures: (1) scoping and screening, which identifies the systems, structures, and components that fall within the scope of the license renewal process; (2) aging management for buried piping and tanks; and (3) aging management for fire protection. We also found that NRC generally followed its documented procedures when conducting its reviews of the following environmental elements: (1) assessing whether there was new and significant information for two generic environmental issues; (2) evaluating applicants' assessments of the potential environmental impacts of two site-specific issues; and (3) evaluating applicants' severe accident mitigation alternatives analyses.[52]

NRC Generally Followed Documented Procedures When Evaluating the Safety Elements of the Applications We Reviewed

NRC generally followed its documented procedures when reviewing selected safety elements in the eight license renewal applications we reviewed. We did not evaluate the adequacy or the substance of NRC's reviews or the quality of its procedures. As part of our review, we examined three elements of the scoping and screening review—an evaluation of an applicant's methodology and results for identifying the set of structures and components that are within the scope of license renewal and subject to aging management review—and determined that

---

[51]We reviewed a nonprobability sample of eight license renewal applications, the results of which are not representative of the entirety of NRC's reviews. Thus, our results are not generalizable to all license renewal reviews but provide examples of safety and environmental review elements that NRC reviewed as part of its license renewal process for these applications. See appendix III for additional information regarding the characteristics of the nuclear power reactors included in our review.

[52]To facilitate its environmental reviews, NRC regulations establish its findings on environmental issues for license renewal. See 10 C.F.R. pt. 51, subpt. A, app. B. A subset of these issues are labeled "category 1" and have been determined (1) to apply to either all reactors or those reactors having similar characteristics; (2) have a specific significance level of impact on the environment; and (3) do not warrant the implementation of site-specific efforts to mitigate any potentially adverse impacts. If no new and significant information is identified for these category 1 issues, then they are not required to be evaluated on a site-specific basis as part of the license renewal process.

NRC staff generally followed the agency's documented procedures for reviewing these elements:

- *Scoping and screening methodology:* According to NRC's documented procedures,[53] NRC staff are expected to review, among other things, the applicant's scoping and screening methodology to determine whether it is sufficiently comprehensive to identify the systems, structures, and components that are within the scope of license renewal and the structures and components requiring an aging management review. We found that NRC staff consistently followed the agency's documented procedures for reviewing the scoping and screening methodology sections for each of the eight license renewal applications we reviewed.
- *Plant-level scoping results:* According to the procedures,[54] NRC staff are expected to also verify the applicant's scoping results to determine if the applicant properly identified the systems, structures, and components that fall within the scope of license renewal. To do so, NRC staff review selected systems, structures, and components that the applicant did not identify in the scoping results to verify that those systems, structures, and components do not have any functions covered under the license renewal requirements. We found that NRC staff consistently followed the agency's documented procedures for reviewing the plant-level scoping results sections for each of the eight license renewal applications we reviewed.
- *Scoping and screening inspection:* As part of the license renewal process, NRC inspectors are expected to conduct a scoping and screening inspection, through on-site reviews and walk-downs of selected areas, to verify that the applicant has adequately identified and documented all the systems, structures, and components as required. Further, the NRC inspectors are to verify that there is reasonable assurance that the applicant has adequately documented all the identified passive and long-lived systems, structures, and components requiring an aging management review. According to our review, NRC staff consistently followed the agency's documented

---

[53]NRC, *Standard Review Plan for Review of License Renewal Applications for Nuclear Power Plants*, NUREG-1800, Initial Report (Washington, D.C.: July 2001), 2.1-1 and NRC, *Standard Review Plan for Review of License Renewal Applications for Nuclear Power Plants*, NUREG-1800, Revision 1 (Washington, D.C.: September 2005), 2.1-1.

[54]NUREG-1800, Initial Report (2001), 2.2-1 and NUREG-1800, Revision 1 (2005), 2.2-1.

procedures[55] for the scoping and screening inspections for three of the eight license renewal applications included in our sample. However, we found that NRC staff reviews were partially consistent in following the agency's documented procedures for the five remaining license renewal reviews. Specifically, we did not identify explicit references in NRC inspection reports or final safety reports that documented that agency staff had followed a procedure to include certain components in their inspection sample while conducting their scoping and screening inspection reviews for Columbia, Millstone Unit 3, Pilgrim, Shearon Harris, and Wolf Creek. According to NRC officials, agency staff did not explicitly state in their reports that they had included the specific components in their inspection sample, but that those components were part of the staff's inspections.[56]

We also examined the consistency of NRC's reviews with the agency's documented procedures for another safety element of the license renewal process: aging management program inspections. Per agency guidance, NRC staff are expected to conduct aging management inspections during the license renewal review to verify that the systems, structures, and components the applicant has identified as being subject to an aging management review already have, or will have, aging management programs. During the inspections, NRC staff also are to verify that the current and planned aging management programs will ensure that the negative effects of aging will be managed so that there is reasonable assurance that the intended functions of the systems, structures, and components will be maintained as the reactor continues to operate beyond its original operating license. According to our review, the aging management program inspections for Columbia and Monticello were

---

[55]NRC, *License Renewal Inspection*, Inspection Procedure 71002 (Washington, D.C.: September 2000), 3 and NRC, *License Renewal Inspection*, Inspection Procedure 71002, Revision 1 (Washington, D.C.: February 2005), 2.

[56]In response to our review, NRC officials told us they have begun an evaluation of whether specific guidance is needed to provide additional clarity for agency staff in documenting license renewal inspections. Specifically, agency officials said our review results indicate that license renewal inspection reports may not contain a level of documentation that is descriptive and explicit enough for a reader to understand what inspection objectives were completed. NRC officials stated that, as a first step, they have performed an assessment of the agency's guidance for documenting inspection results. Next, NRC officials plan to review prior license renewal inspection reports to determine if those reports provide at least the same level of documentation provided by other types of NRC inspection reports. Agency officials estimated they would complete this evaluation by the end of 2013.

consistent with agency procedures.[57] However, we found that the NRC reviews for the other six license renewal applications were partially consistent with the agency's documented procedures. Specifically, we did not identify explicit references in the NRC inspection reports or final safety reports that documented that NRC staff had (1) consistently conducted interviews with site staff or (2) the opportunity to perform part of their walk-downs during a reactor outage while conducting their aging management reviews and program inspections for Duane Arnold, Millstone Unit 3, Pilgrim, Shearon Harris, Virgil C. Summer, and Wolf Creek.[58] According to NRC officials, the reports did not explicitly state that interviews were conducted for all of the aging management reviews and program inspections, but that the agency staff interviewed the site staff in charge of each aging management program as part of their inspections. In addition, NRC officials said that it was not always possible to conduct a walk-down during unit outages for some of the reactors we reviewed. For example, NRC staff could not conduct walk-downs during unit outages for Duane Arnold, Shearon Harris, Millstone Unit 3, Pilgrim, and Virgil C. Summer because the schedules for the inspections and unit outages did not align. NRC officials stated that agency staff conducted the walk-downs during the next scheduled unit outage for the Shearon Harris and Virgil C. Summer reactors and documented their review in a separate inspection report.[59] We reviewed the separate inspection reports for both Shearon Harris and Virgil C. Summer and confirmed that agency staff documented that they had conducted the walk-downs during the next unit outage.

---

[57]Inspection Procedure 71002 (2000), 3 and Inspection Procedure 71002, Revision 1 (2005), 2.

[58]According to NRC documents, NRC staff are not required to perform part of their walk-downs during a unit outage. However, the documents state that NRC staff should, if possible, conduct a part of this inspection during a unit outage because this will allow for visual observation of certain components that are inaccessible during normal reactor operations, such as those components located inside containment or in high-radiation areas.

[59]According to NRC officials, walkdowns similar to those performed at Shearon Harris and Virgil C. Summer were not conducted for Duane Arnold, Millstone (Unit 3), and Pilgrim. The officials stated that, per agency guidance, walkdowns during unit outages are optional for aging management program inspections and that NRC staff are expected to review areas not accessible during unit outages as part of other NRC inspections that are done outside of the license renewal process.

GAO-13-493 NRC's License Renewal Process

In addition, we examined the consistency of NRC reviews with the agency's documented procedures for two aging management programs—(1) buried piping and tanks inspection and (2) fire protection—and found that NRC's documented actions for those reviews were generally consistent with the agency's documented procedures.

- *Buried piping and tanks inspection program:* The buried piping and tanks inspection program relies on preventive measures, frequency of pipe excavation, and operating experience to manage the effects of the loss of material that forms the pipes and tanks from various types of corrosion. In some circumstances, the loss of such material as a result of corrosion could lead to radioactive leaks. According to NRC documents, the effectiveness of the buried piping and tanks inspection program should be verified to evaluate an applicant's inspection frequency and operating experience with buried components and ensure that the effects of any potential corrosion have not resulted in radioactive leaks from the buried piping or tanks.[60] From our review, we found that, for seven of the eight license renewal applications included in our sample, NRC consistently followed the agency's documented procedures[61] for reviewing an applicant's buried piping and tanks inspection program. The NRC review for Millstone Unit 3 was partially consistent with documented agency procedures. Of the five steps outlined in NRC's procedures for reviewing an applicant's buried piping and tanks inspection program, agency staff explicitly stated in their audit reports and final safety reports that they had followed four of them. However, it was not clear whether agency staff consistently followed a fifth procedural step to review both plant-specific and industry-wide operating experience as part of their review. Specifically, we found references in NRC's audit report and final safety report for the Millstone Unit 3 review that agency staff reviewed plant-specific operating experience, but agency staff did not explicitly state that they reviewed industry-wide operating experience to determine whether lessons learned identified at other reactors could be applied to Millstone's efforts to manage the aging of

---

[60]The buried piping and tanks inspection program for the reactors included in our nonprobability sample were reviewed by NRC staff using either the 2001 or 2005 versions of NRC's *Generic Aging Lessons Learned Report.* In December 2010, NRC issued its revised *Generic Aging Lessons Learned Report,* which included updates to the buried piping and tanks inspection program. The program is now referred to as the buried and underground piping and tanks program.

[61]NUREG-1800, Initial Report (2001), 3.1.3 and NUREG-1800, Revision 1 (2005), 3.1.3.

buried piping and tanks. According to NRC officials, it is a standard practice for agency staff to review both plant-specific and industry-wide operating experience. Further, those officials said that NRC staff's audit review plan included plant-specific and industry-wide operating experience as areas expected to be reviewed by agency staff during the Millstone Unit 3 review.

- *Fire protection program:* According to NRC safety review guidance, the fire protection program is intended to manage the effects of loss of material and cracking, increased hardness, shrinkage, and loss of strength on the intended functions for fire protection features and components, such as fire barrier penetration seals, fire barrier walls, and all fire-rated doors that perform a fire barrier function. NRC staff are to review the applicant's fire protection program to determine whether the potential effects of aging are managed by periodic visual inspections performed during walk-downs, tests, and engineering evaluations to ensure that the capability of the fire protection systems will be maintained during the period of the reactor's extended operation. We found that NRC reviews for seven of the eight license renewal applications in our sample consistently followed the agency's documented procedures[62] for reviewing the applicant's fire protection program. Our review found that the NRC review for Millstone Unit 3 was partially consistent with agency procedures. Of the five steps outlined in NRC's procedures for reviewing an applicant's fire protection program, agency staff explicitly stated in NRC audit reports and final safety reports that they had followed four of them. As with the buried piping and tanks inspection program, however, it was not clear whether NRC staff consistently followed a fifth procedural step to review both plant-specific and industry-wide operating experience for the fire protection program as part of the Millstone Unit 3 review because agency staff did not explicitly state that they had done so. According to NRC officials, it is a standard practice to review both plant-specific and industry-wide operating experience. Further, the officials said that the NRC staff's audit review plan included plant-specific and industry-wide operating experience as areas expected to be reviewed by agency staff during the review of the fire protection program for Millstone Unit 3.

---

[62]NUREG-1800, Initial Report (2001), 3.1.3 and NUREG-1800, Revision 1 (2005), 3.1.3.

NRC Generally Followed Its Procedures When Evaluating the Environmental Elements of the Applications We Reviewed

We found that NRC generally followed its documented procedures when reviewing selected environmental elements for the eight license renewal applications included in our sample. We did not evaluate the adequacy or the substance of NRC's reviews or the quality of its procedures. As part of our review, we examined selected elements from: (1) NRC's reviews of new and significant information for two generic issues; (2) NRC's evaluation of applicants' assessments of the potential environmental impacts for two site-specific issues; and (3) NRC's evaluation of the applicants' severe accident mitigation alternatives analyses.

As part of our review of the consistency of NRC staff evaluations for new and significant information with the agency's documented procedures, we examined NRC's reviews for two generic environmental issues—cold shock and gas supersaturation. According to the agency's 1996 environmental regulations, reactor owners are to include in their license renewal applications any new and significant information they are aware of regarding the potential environmental impacts of license renewal. As discussed earlier in this report, NRC staff are also expected to look for and consider any new and significant information for both generic and site-specific environmental issues when conducting their reviews. For generic environmental issues, NRC procedures call for agency staff to, among other things, review the previous information and conclusions reached for each issue and then determine if there is any new environmental information that should be considered. If any new information is identified, NRC staff are expected to evaluate the information to determine whether it changes the agency's prior conclusions about the significance level of the environmental issue. We reviewed whether NRC reports documented that agency staff had followed NRC's procedures for evaluating new and significant information on cold shock and gas supersaturation. We found that the agency's reviews for cold shock and gas supersaturation were generally consistent with the agency's documented procedures.

- *Cold shock:* Cold shock is a form of thermal stress caused by exposure to a sudden decrease of water temperature that adversely affects the metabolism and behavior of an aquatic organism and can lead to its death.[63] According to its generic environmental impact statement for license renewal, NRC has found that cold shock has been satisfactorily mitigated at operating nuclear reactors and is not expected to be a problem if the reactor operates for another 20 years beyond its original operating license. As the issue applies to all reactors, NRC has considered it a generic issue that will be evaluated further only if new and significant information is identified. We found that NRC staff reviews consistently followed the agency's documented procedures[64] for seven of the eight license renewal applications included in our sample. We found that NRC's review for the Wolf Creek application was partially consistent with the agency's documented procedures. Of the five possible procedures to follow when conducting a review for new and significant information on cold shock, we found that NRC staff consistently followed one procedure, and because staff did not identify any new and significant information, three other procedures accordingly were not completed. We did not, however, see an explicit reference in the source documents we reviewed to NRC staff having followed a fifth procedure to search for new information related to regulations affecting cooling systems. According to NRC officials, agency staff are given flexibility, as prescribed by NRC's environmental standard review plan, in conducting their searches for new information, and they also can leverage information from other sections of the environmental review and associated supplemental environmental impact statement, particularly issues related to how the continued operation of the reactor will affect land use, water quality, and water use.

- *Gas supersaturation (gas bubble disease)*: Gas supersaturation occurs when concentrations of dissolved gases in water exceed the normal saturation limit. When gas supersaturation occurs, it can lead to a condition known as gas bubble disease, which can cause swelling and hemorrhaging in the tissues of aquatic organisms that

---

[63]According to an NRC document, cold shock occurs when organisms that have been acclimated to warm water, such as in a nuclear power plant's discharge canal in winter, are exposed to sudden temperature decreases when artificial heating ceases. Such situations could occur if a single-reactor plant suddenly shut down in winter or if winds or currents shifted a thermal plume occupied by aquatic organisms seeking warm water.

[64]NUREG-1555, Supplement 1, 4.1-4.

can lead to behavioral abnormalities or death.[65] According to NRC's generic environmental impact statement for license renewal, the agency has found that gas supersaturation has been satisfactorily mitigated across reactors and is not expected to be a problem if a reactor operates for another 20 years beyond its original operating license. We found that NRC staff consistently followed the agency's documented procedures for seven of the eight license renewal applications included in our sample. We found that NRC's review for the Wolf Creek application was partially consistent with the agency's documented procedures.[66] Of the five possible procedures to follow when conducting a review for new and significant information on gas supersaturation, we found that NRC staff consistently followed one procedure, and because they did not identify any new and significant information, accordingly, three other procedures were not completed. We did not, however, see an explicit reference in the source documents we reviewed to NRC staff having followed a fifth procedure to search for new information related to regulations affecting cooling systems. According to NRC officials, NRC staff are given flexibility, as prescribed by NRC's environmental standard review plan, in conducting their searches for new information, and they also can leverage information from other sections of the environmental review and associated supplemental environmental impact statement, particularly issues related to how the continued operation of the reactor will affect land use, water quality, and water use.

As part of our review, we also examined the consistency of NRC staff actions with agency procedures for reviews of site-specific environmental issues, termed "category 2" issues. These environmental issues differ from the generic environmental issues identified by NRC because agency regulations preclude a generic determination of potential impacts. For these site-specific issues, the license renewal applicant must provide a

---

[65]According to an NRC document, rapid heating of water in a nuclear power plant's condenser cooling system decreases the solubility and increases saturation levels of dissolved gases. The supersaturation of nitrogen gas could lead to incidents of gas bubble disease in the discharge areas of nuclear power plants. Gas bubble disease is a condition that occurs when aquatic organisms are exposed to water with high partial pressures of certain gases (usually nitrogen) and then subsequently are exposed to water with lower partial pressures of the same gases. Dissolved gases (especially nitrogen) within the tissues of these organisms may come out of solution and form embolisms, or bubbles, within the affected tissues, most noticeably the eyes and fins.

[66]NUREG-1555, Supplement 1, 4.1-4.

site-specific impact analysis in its environmental report and, per agency guidance, NRC staff are expected to perform and document their independent review of the issue in a supplemental environmental impact statement. Specifically, we examined whether NRC reports documented that agency staff had followed NRC's procedures for two such site-specific environmental issues: (1) threatened or endangered species and (2) off-site land use during operations.

- *Threatened or endangered species:* As part of the license renewal process, NRC staff are expected to conduct an analysis that considers the impacts of a reactor's continued operations on threatened or endangered species and also examines reasonable and prudent alternatives for avoiding or reducing potentially adverse impacts.[67] NRC procedures call for agency staff to, among other things, review potential site-specific impacts of continued operations on threatened or endangered species and determine whether any potential environmental impacts may have adverse effects on those species or critical habitat. If any potential site-specific effects are identified, then NRC staff are expected to consult with relevant federal agencies and, if necessary, initiate a biological assessment to address how those species or critical habitat may be affected. We found that NRC reports documented that agency staff consistently followed NRC's documented procedures[68] for evaluating the potential environmental impacts of continued operations on threatened or endangered species for each of the eight license renewal applications we reviewed.
- *Off-site land use during operations:* According to NRC regulations, significant changes in land use may be associated with population and tax revenue changes resulting from license renewal. Further, given that there are many site-specific variables related to how off-site land will be used if a reactor continues to operate beyond its original operating license, NRC staff are expected to examine this issue on a site-by-site basis to determine whether any potential environmental impacts may occur. NRC procedures call for agency staff to, among

---

[67]Under the Endangered Species Act of 1973, as amended, all federal agencies must, among other things, utilize their authorities to carry out programs for the conservation of threatened and endangered species, including those cases where proposed federal actions may affect threatened or endangered species. In each license renewal environmental review, NRC officials stated that the agency consults with the U.S. Fish and Wildlife Service and/or the National Marine Fisheries Service.

[68]NUREG-1555, Supplement 1, 4.6.1-6.

other things, obtain site-specific information to determine the potential scope of off-site land use impacts and evaluate whether those impacts may be large enough to require further analysis. If agency staff find that the effects of the potential impacts may be more than minor, then they are expected to consider and evaluate potential mitigation measures or alternatives that might reduce or eliminate the potentially adverse impacts. We found that NRC reports documented that agency staff consistently followed NRC's documented procedures[69] for evaluating the potential environmental impacts of off-site land use during continued operations for each of the eight license renewal applications we reviewed.

We also examined the consistency of NRC staff reviews of the applicants' severe accident mitigation alternatives analyses with the agency's documented procedures. NRC regulations state that alternatives to mitigate severe accidents must be considered for all reactors that have not previously considered such alternatives.[70] Severe accident mitigation alternatives are considered site-specific and thereby require that the applicant conduct a site-specific evaluation that will be reviewed by NRC staff during the license renewal process. The severe accident mitigation alternatives analyses performed in support of license renewal applications typically focus on areas of greatest risk and on measures that could provide the greatest risk reduction in a cost-beneficial fashion. NRC procedures call for agency staff to, among other things, evaluate the potential mitigation alternatives identified by the applicant. Moreover, NRC officials told us that agency staff are expected to determine whether any of the alternatives have been identified as being within the scope of license renewal by being both cost-beneficial and related to aging management. We reviewed the steps NRC staff documented taking to conduct their evaluation of applicants' severe accident mitigation alternatives analyses and found that NRC staff consistently followed the agency's documented procedures[71] for each of the eight license renewal applications included in our sample.

---

[69]NUREG-1555, Supplement 1, 4.4.3-3.

[70]10 C.F.R. § 51.53(c)(3)(ii)(L) (2013).

[71]NUREG-1555, Supplement 1, 5.1.1-6.

Knowledgeable Stakeholders Identified Various Perceived Strengths and Weaknesses in the License Renewal Process, and Some Suggested Potential Improvements

The 15 stakeholders we interviewed who were knowledgeable on NRC's license renewal process provided their views on various perceived strengths and weaknesses of the process, with some suggesting potential improvements to the process. Stakeholders most often identified the technical knowledge of NRC staff and the thoroughness of the agency's reviews as perceived strengths of the license renewal process. Stakeholders also identified a range of perceived weaknesses of the license renewal process, including claims that its scope is too narrow and that its public hearing process is flawed and inhibits meaningful public participation. Some stakeholders we interviewed suggested potential changes to improve the license renewal process, including broadening the scope of NRC's reviews and modifying aspects of the public hearing process.

Stakeholders Most Often Identified the Technical Knowledge of NRC Staff and the Thoroughness of Reviews as Perceived Strengths

The 15 stakeholders we interviewed identified a number of perceived strengths of NRC's license renewal process. Overall, all eight industry and ACRS stakeholders and one state government stakeholder said the license renewal process is generally effective at accomplishing its safety and environmental goals, and all but one of those same stakeholders plus one public interest group stakeholder said the scope of the process is sufficient.[72] More specifically, among the 15 stakeholders we interviewed, four strengths were identified by three or more stakeholders as follows:[73]

- First, more than half of the stakeholders we interviewed (9 of 15) identified the technical knowledge of NRC's staff as a strength of the license renewal process. Several of these stakeholders said that NRC staff is knowledgeable and experienced in the issues they review and that this leads to a more efficient review process.
- Second, about half of the stakeholders (7 of 15) identified as a strength what they said was the thoroughness of the process that NRC uses to review license renewal applications. A few of these stakeholders highlighted the number of different reviews performed by agency staff, including on-site audits and inspections, and the external review performed by ACRS. One stakeholder stated that NRC

---

[72]One industry stakeholder who said the license renewal process is generally effective at accomplishing its safety and environmental goals said that the scope of the license renewal process is too broad.

[73]Three stakeholders we interviewed said NRC's license renewal process has no significant strengths.

requires applicants to make changes to their applications and proposed license renewal programs—in their view, it is not a "rubber stamp" process.

- Third, about a third of the stakeholders (6 of 15) pointed to the quality of NRC's license renewal guidance as another strength of the agency's process. A few of these stakeholders said that because NRC's guidance documents clearly define the agency's expectations for applicants and staff reviewers, the documents make the license renewal process more efficient and focus discussion on key issues. One stakeholder noted that NRC's standard review plan is particularly important since it helps agency staff with less experience understand what they should be looking for during their license renewal reviews.

- Fourth, a few stakeholders (4 of 15) identified as a strength how safety review guidance has evolved over time to account for new information and lessons learned from previous license renewal reviews. One of these stakeholders emphasized that NRC has actively sought new information and, in this stakeholder's view, has regularly incorporated that information into its safety review guidance.

Stakeholders Identified Some Perceived Weaknesses, Including the Scope of the Review and a Flawed Public Hearing Process

The 15 stakeholders we interviewed also identified a number of perceived weaknesses in NRC's license renewal process. Overall, 5 of 7 public interest group and state government stakeholders said the license renewal process is generally ineffective at accomplishing its goals, and the same stakeholders said the scope of the process is too narrow.[74] More specifically, among the 15 stakeholders we interviewed, two weaknesses were identified by five or more stakeholders as follows:[75]

- First, about a third of the stakeholders we interviewed (6 of 15) identified as a weakness what they said was the overly narrow scope of the license renewal process. Some of these stakeholders said that issues the public thinks are relevant to license renewal, such as emergency planning and security, fall outside the scope of the license renewal process. One stakeholder said license renewal reviews should have a broader scope so that NRC can ensure at license renewal that reactors meet current safety requirements in all areas.

---

[74]One public interest stakeholder said the license renewal process is effective in some ways but not effective in other ways, and said the scope of the process is sufficient.

[75]One stakeholder we interviewed said that NRC's license renewal process has no significant weaknesses.

Another stakeholder provided the view that license renewal should be an opportunity to consider a wide range of safety and environmental issues beyond the negative effects of aging since license renewal allows a reactor to operate for up to an additional 20 years.

- Second, a third of stakeholders (5 of 15) identified as an additional weakness of NRC's license renewal process what in their view is the agency's flawed public hearing process for considering challenges to license renewal applications. One of these stakeholders pointed to the limited time the public has to file challenges to a license renewal application (i.e., 60 days after the agency has published notice of the opportunity for a public hearing on a license renewal application), and other stakeholders highlighted hearing procedures that they believe put the public at a disadvantage compared with license renewal applicants. Some stakeholders said they believe NRC's public hearing process inhibits meaningful public participation in the license renewal process.

The following five other perceived weaknesses of the license renewal process were identified by 3 stakeholders each:

- NRC does not require reactor owners with previously-renewed licenses to revise their programs for managing the negative effects of aging when NRC updates its license renewal guidance;
- NRC reviews of license renewal applications are not thorough enough;
- NRC reviews of license renewal applications can be excessive and address issues that fall outside the scope of the license renewal process;
- NRC staff are not open to new information brought forward by stakeholders; and
- NRC does not require applicants to implement cost-beneficial upgrades identified during the license renewal environmental review if those upgrades are not related to aging.

Some Stakeholders Suggested Changes to the License Renewal Process, Including Broadening Its Scope and Modifying the Public Hearing Process

Some of the 15 stakeholders we interviewed suggested potential changes to improve NRC's license renewal process. Six changes were suggested by three or more stakeholders.[76] We asked NRC officials for the agency's position on these suggested changes. The six changes suggested by three or more stakeholders and NRC officials' explanations of the agency's position on those potential changes were as follows:

- Six stakeholders suggested NRC modify its public hearing process for considering challenges to license renewal applications. These stakeholders identified a number of modifications NRC could make, including increasing the amount of time the public has to file challenges and providing funding to public groups to present their cases. According to NRC officials, the NRC Commissioners determined in 2004 that the 60 days the public has to file challenges is adequate and that the public effectively has more time due to (1) internet notice of preapplication meetings, (2) the availability of the license renewal application prior to the notice of opportunity for hearing, and (3) *Federal Register* or internet notice of the filing of an application and acceptance of the application for docketing.[77] Also, NRC is prohibited by law from providing funding to parties, such as public groups, intervening in NRC's regulatory or adjudicatory proceedings to present their cases.[78]
- Five stakeholders suggested that NRC expand the scope of the license renewal process to consider issues beyond the negative effects of aging, such as emergency planning and spent fuel storage. According to NRC officials, when the agency issued the original license renewal rule in 1991 and amended it in 1995, the NRC Commissioners determined that NRC's ongoing regulatory processes

---

[76]Five stakeholders we interviewed said that they do not believe NRC needs to make significant changes to the license renewal process.

[77]The NRC Commissioners considered the amount of time the public has to file challenges in 2004 when it revised its adjudicatory process. See 69 Fed. Reg. 2182, 2199 (Jan. 14, 2004). In the proposed rule, the NRC Commissioners solicited views on appropriate time frames for allowing petitions to be filed based on a notice of opportunity for hearing. To address comments that a 45-day period was insufficient, the NRC Commissioners decided to provide a 60-day period for most actions.

[78]See Energy and Water Development Appropriations Act for FY 1993, Pub. L. No. 102-377 § 502 (1992) ("None of the funds in this Act or subsequent Energy and Water Development Appropriations Acts shall be used to pay the expenses of, or otherwise compensate, parties intervening in regulatory or adjudicatory proceedings funded in such Acts.").

were sufficient to ensure that a reactor would operate safely under a renewed license, with the possible exception of age-related degradation.[79] As a result, NRC made managing the negative effects of aging the primary focus of the license renewal process. NRC officials noted that the agency is reviewing public comments on whether or not to broaden the scope of the license renewal process as it considers the process it will use to review applications to renew reactor operating licenses for a second time. NRC officials stated that a determination is in development by staff and is expected to be completed by the end of fiscal year 2013.

- Three stakeholders suggested that NRC improve the public's access to information used in the agency's license renewal reviews. For example, one stakeholder said that the public should be allowed to listen to all conversations between agency staff and an applicant regarding a license renewal application. According to NRC officials, the agency provides the public access to, among other things, any information that NRC considers during a license renewal review if that information was necessary for the agency to make its license renewal decision. In addition, NRC officials said that communications from applicants are placed in the agency's publicly available recordkeeping system, unless they are withheld in accordance with agency regulations.[80]

- Three stakeholders suggested that NRC should change its submission requirements for license renewal applications so that reactor owners have to submit a fully complete application at the beginning of the license renewal process. According to NRC officials, the agency requires applicants to submit applications that are sufficiently complete for NRC to conduct its review. However, they noted that the agency allows applicants to amend their applications and that applicants sometimes do so both in response to NRC questions and at their own initiation.

- Three stakeholders suggested that NRC should require reactor owners with previously renewed licenses to meet new standards when NRC updates its license renewal guidance. According to NRC officials, the standards in the agency's license renewal guidance reflect one but not the only way for an applicant to meet license

---

[79]See 56 Fed. Reg. 64,943 (Dec. 13, 1991) and 60 Fed. Reg. 22,461 (May 8, 1995).

[80]10 C.F.R. § 2.390 (2013).

renewal requirements. Because standards in the guidance documents are not requirements, NRC does not require reactor owners with previously-renewed licenses to update their programs for managing the negative effects of aging when the agency updates its guidance. However, according to agency officials, NRC expects these owners to review updates to the agency's license renewal guidance and consider whether they need to make changes to their programs as a result.

- Three stakeholders suggested that NRC should require reactor owners to implement all cost beneficial upgrades identified during the license renewal environmental review, regardless of whether those upgrades are related to aging. According to NRC officials, because the scope of the license renewal process is focused primarily on managing the negative effects of aging, the agency has decided not to require reactor owners as part of the license renewal process to implement cost beneficial upgrades identified during the environmental review that are not related to aging. However, the officials noted that those upgrades could be considered through NRC's "backfit" process, which generally requires NRC to assure reactor owners that requirements placed on them will change only when warranted from a public health and safety standpoint.[81]

Agency Comments

We provided a draft copy of this report to the Executive Director for Operations of NRC for review and comment. NRC provided written comments on the draft report, which are reproduced in appendix IV, and technical comments, which we incorporated into the report as appropriate. In its comments, NRC neither agreed nor disagreed with our findings.

---

[81]NRC's "backfit rule" requires, in order to impose new requirements on existing licensees, that NRC determine that the new requirements would result in a substantial increase in the overall protection of public health and safety or common defense and security and that this increased protection justifies the cost of implementation. 10 C.F.R. § 50.109(a)(3) (2013). Backfit is defined in 10 C.F.R. § 50.109(a)(1) as the modification of or addition to systems, structures, components, or design of a facility; or the design approval or manufacturing license for a facility; or the procedures or organization required to design, construct or operate a facility; any of which may result from a new or amended provision in NRC's regulations or the imposition of a regulatory staff position interpreting NRC's regulations that is either new or different from a previously applicable staff position, relative to specific dates, such as issuance of licenses. The backfit rule requires a backfit analysis demonstrating that the new or changed requirement is a substantial increase in overall protection unless NRC finds that a backfit is needed to ensure that protection of public health and safety is adequate, or in other limited situations. 10 C.F.R. § 50.109(a)(3)-(4).

As agreed with your offices, unless you publicly announce the contents of this report earlier, we plan no further distribution until 30 days from the report date. At that time, we will send copies to NRC, the appropriate congressional committees, and other interested parties. In addition, this report will be available at no charge on the GAO website at http://www.gao.gov.

If you or your staff members have any questions about this report, please contact me at (202) 512-3841 or ruscof@gao.gov. Contact points for our Offices of Congressional Relations and Public Affairs may be found on the last page of this report. Key contributors to this report are listed in appendix V.

Frank Rusco
Director, Natural Resources and Environment

List of Requesters

The Honorable Barbara Boxer
Chairman
Committee on Environment and Public Works
United States Senate

The Honorable Sheldon Whitehouse
Chairman
Subcommittee on Oversight
Committee on Environment and Public Works
United States Senate

The Honorable Bernard Sanders
United States Senate

The Honorable Edward J. Markey
House of Representatives

Appendix I: Objectives, Scope, and Methodology

Our review provides information on: (1) the scope of the Nuclear Regulatory Commission's (NRC) license renewal process for commercial nuclear power reactors; (2) the extent to which NRC updates the safety and environmental review guidance used in the license renewal process; (3) the extent to which NRC follows the agency's documented license renewal procedures; and (4) knowledgeable stakeholders' views on the strengths and weaknesses in the license renewal process and suggestions, if any, for improving the process. To address these objectives and better understand NRC's license renewal process, we reviewed relevant NRC documents and met with officials from NRC and representatives from the nuclear power industry, public interest groups, and others.

During the course of our review, we interviewed NRC officials from the Office of General Counsel, Office of New Reactors, Office of Nuclear Reactor Regulation, and Office of Nuclear Regulatory Research in headquarters. We also interviewed officials from NRC's Office of the Inspector General (OIG), NRC's Atomic Safety and Licensing Board, and the Advisory Committee on Reactor Safeguards (ACRS), as well as NRC officials in Region I and the resident inspectors at the two nuclear power plants we visited. In addition, we interviewed representatives from the Nuclear Energy Institute, the Union of Concerned Scientists, and other groups and individuals to discuss their views on NRC's license renewal process.

Specifically, to describe the scope of NRC's license renewal process, we reviewed relevant laws and NRC regulations, including the Atomic Energy Act of 1954 as amended and 10 C.F.R. Parts 2, 51, and 54, as well as relevant NRC guidance documents. In addition, we interviewed NRC officials to gain a further understanding of the license renewal process and how the process has changed over time. We also visited a nonprobability sample of two nuclear power plants—Millstone Power Station in Connecticut and the Pilgrim Nuclear Power Station in Massachusetts—to interview plant representatives about their experience with the license renewal process and to observe programs implemented at the sites following license renewal. Because this was a nonprobability sample, the information we gathered from these site visits is not generalizable to all nuclear power plants but provides important illustrative information. We selected these sites to capture a variety of characteristics, including sites that had gone through the license renewal process, at least one site that was operating under a renewed license beyond its initial 40-year operating period, and at least one site that was

the subject of a public hearing concerning a challenge to its license
renewal application.

To determine the extent to which NRC updates the safety and
environmental review guidance used in the license renewal process, we
examined NRC documents on its guidance revision process and reviewed
changes made to license renewal guidance documents, including the
standard review plans for license renewal safety and environmental
reviews, the *Generic Aging Lessons Learned Report*, and the *Generic
Environmental Impact Statement for License Renewal of Nuclear Plants*.
We also reviewed NRC documents describing the process for revising
license renewal environmental review regulations and guidance and
interviewed NRC officials about the process.

To determine the extent to which NRC followed the agency's documented
license renewal procedures, we selected a nonprobability sample of the
safety and environmental review elements that are assessed as part of
NRC's license renewal process. We selected the elements to examine
based on a review of GAO and NRC OIG reports, NRC guidance, license
renewal documents from site visits, and input from some of the
stakeholders we interviewed. In addition, we randomly selected some of
the review elements for inclusion in our sample. To identify the agency's
documented procedures for reviewing the elements included in our
sample, we examined NRC's standard review plans for license renewal
safety and environmental reviews and its license renewal inspection
protocols. We then identified the actions NRC staff took to review the
selected elements, as documented in NRC audit reports, inspection
reports, and final safety and environmental reports, for a nonprobability
sample of eight license renewal applications. Our nonprobability sample
consisted of the following license renewal applications: Columbia
Generating Station, Duane Arnold Energy Center, Millstone Power
Station (Unit 3), Monticello Nuclear Generating Plant, Pilgrim Nuclear
Power Station, Shearon Harris Nuclear Power Plant, Virgil C. Summer
Nuclear Station, and Wolf Creek Generating Station.[1] We selected this
sample to capture a variety of characteristics, including reactors from
different NRC regions, and reactors whose license renewal applications
were reviewed using different versions of NRC's safety and

---

[1]Because this was a nonprobability sample, our results are not generalizable to all license
renewal reviews but provide examples of safety and environmental review elements that
NRC reviewed as part of its license renewal process.

environmental review guidance. Two GAO analysts independently
compared NRC staff's documented actions with the agency's
documented procedures to assess the level of consistency for the review
elements in our sample. They then rated the staff's documented actions
as compared with the agency's documented procedures as being
consistent, partially consistent, not consistent, or not applicable. When
their review ratings differed, they discussed the differences and agreed
on a final assessment. We then spoke with NRC officials about the
instances where the staff's documented actions were rated as either
partially consistent or not consistent in order to determine whether NRC
had additional information that could illustrate the extent to which the
agency's procedures were followed in a consistent manner. During our
review, we did not evaluate the adequacy or substance of NRC's review
actions or the quality of its documented license renewal procedures.

To describe knowledgeable stakeholders' views on strengths and
weaknesses in NRC's license renewal process, we summarized the
results of semistructured interviews with stakeholders knowledgeable of
the license renewal process. We first identified 106 knowledgeable
stakeholders by reviewing the results of a literature search, prior GAO
reports, congressional and NRC hearings, and recommendations from
officials with NRC and representatives from the Nuclear Energy Institute,
the Union of Concerned Scientists, and others. From this list, we then
used a multistep process to select 15 stakeholders. To ensure coverage
and a range of perspectives, we selected stakeholders from the following:

- industry, including officials from five of the eight nuclear power plants
  whose license renewal applications were part of the nonprobability
  sample for our consistency review;
- public interest groups, including representatives from the National
  Legal Scholars Firm, Pilgrim Watch, Public Justice, and the Union of
  Concerned Scientists;
- state governments, including officials from the States of New York and
  Vermont and the Commonwealth of Massachusetts; and

- ACRS, a body of nuclear, engineering, and safety experts appointed by the NRC Commissioners that is independent of the NRC staff and reports directly to the NRC Commissioners.[2]

We conducted semistructured interviews with the 15 selected stakeholders using a standard set of questions and analyzed their responses, grouping them into overall themes.[3] We summarized the results of our analysis and then asked NRC officials for the agency's position on potential changes to the license renewal process that were suggested by multiple stakeholders. Not all of the stakeholders answered all of our questions. The views expressed by stakeholders do not represent the views of GAO.

We conducted this performance audit from May 2012 to May 2013 in accordance with generally accepted government auditing standards. Those standards require that we plan and perform the audit to obtain sufficient, appropriate evidence to provide a reasonable basis for our findings and conclusions based on our audit objectives. We believe that the evidence obtained provides a reasonable basis for our findings and conclusions based on our audit objectives.

---

[2]ACRS is established in statute. The committee has four primary purposes: (1) to review and report on safety studies and reactor facility license and license renewal applications; (2) to advise the NRC Commissioners on the hazards of proposed and existing production and utilization facilities and the adequacy of proposed safety standards; (3) to initiate reviews of specific generic matters or nuclear facility safety-related items; and (4) to provide advice in the areas of health physics and radiation protection.

[3]During one industry stakeholder interview, the primary stakeholder was joined by two colleagues who provided supporting commentary. However, the three officials, as noted during our interview, expressed a singular view for their group. Therefore, this interview represented the views of one industry stakeholder, not three separate views.

Appendix II: License Renewal Status of Operating Commercial Nuclear Power Reactors as of May 2013

Reactor	State	Date initial operating license issued	License renewal status[a]	Date renewed operating license issued	Date current operating license set to expire
Arkansas Nuclear One, Unit 1	Arkansas	05/21/1974	Renewed	06/20/2001	05/20/2034
Arkansas Nuclear One, Unit 2	Arkansas	09/01/1978	Renewed	06/30/2005	07/17/2038
Beaver Valley Power Station, Unit 1	Pennsylvania	07/02/1976	Renewed	11/05/2009	01/29/2036
Beaver Valley Power Station, Unit 2	Pennsylvania	08/14/1987	Renewed	11/05/2009	05/27/2047
Braidwood Station, Unit 1	Illinois	07/02/1987	Application Expected	N/A	10/17/2026
Braidwood Station, Unit 2	Illinois	05/20/1988	Application Expected	N/A	12/18/2027
Browns Ferry Nuclear Plant, Unit 1	Alabama	12/20/1973	Renewed	05/04/2006	12/20/2033
Browns Ferry Nuclear Plant, Unit 2	Alabama	06/28/1974	Renewed	05/04/2006	06/28/2034
Browns Ferry Nuclear Plant, Unit 3	Alabama	07/02/1976	Renewed	05/04/2006	07/02/2036
Brunswick Steam Electric Plant, Unit 1	North Carolina	09/08/1976	Renewed	06/26/2006	09/08/2036
Brunswick Steam Electric Plant, Unit 2	North Carolina	12/27/1974	Renewed	06/26/2006	12/27/2034
Byron Station, Unit 1	Illinois	02/14/1985	Application Expected	N/A	10/31/2024
Byron Station, Unit 2	Illinois	01/30/1987	Application Expected	N/A	11/06/2026
Callaway Plant	Missouri	10/18/1984	Under Review	N/A	10/18/2024
Calvert Cliffs Nuclear Power Plant, Unit 1	Maryland	07/31/1974	Renewed	03/23/2000	07/31/2034
Calvert Cliffs Nuclear Power Plant, Unit 2	Maryland	08/13/1976	Renewed	03/23/2000	08/13/2036
Catawba Nuclear Station, Unit 1	South Carolina	01/17/1985	Renewed	12/05/2003	12/05/2043
Catawba Nuclear Station, Unit 2	South Carolina	05/15/1986	Renewed	12/05/2003	12/05/2043
Clinton Power Station, Unit 1	Illinois	04/17/1987	Application Expected	N/A	09/29/2026
Columbia Generating Station, Unit 2	Washington State	04/13/1984	Renewed	05/22/2012	12/20/2043
Comanche Peak Steam Electric Station, Unit 1	Texas	04/17/1990	Application Expected	N/A	02/08/2030

Reactor	State	Date initial operating license issued	License renewal status[a]	Date renewed operating license issued	Date current operating license set to expire
Comanche Peak Steam Electric Station, Unit 2	Texas	04/06/1993	Application Expected	N/A	02/02/2033
Cooper Nuclear Station	Nebraska	01/18/1974	Renewed	11/29/2010	01/18/2034
Davis-Besse Nuclear Power Station, Unit 1	Ohio	04/22/1977	Under Review	N/A	04/22/2017
Diablo Canyon Nuclear Power Plant, Unit 1	California	11/02/1984	Under Review	N/A	11/02/2024
Diablo Canyon Nuclear Power Plant, Unit 2	California	08/26/1985	Under Review	N/A	08/26/2025
Donald C. Cook Nuclear Power Plant, Unit 1	Michigan	10/25/1974	Renewed	08/30/2005	10/25/2034
Donald C. Cook Nuclear Power Plant, Unit 2	Michigan	12/23/1977	Renewed	08/30/2005	12/23/2037
Dresden Nuclear Power Station, Unit 2	Illinois	02/20/1991	Renewed	10/28/2004	12/22/2029
Dresden Nuclear Power Station, Unit 3	Illinois	01/12/1971	Renewed	10/28/2004	01/12/2031
Duane Arnold Energy Center	Iowa	02/22/1974	Renewed	12/16/2010	02/21/2034
Edwin I. Hatch Nuclear Plant, Unit 1	Georgia	10/13/1974	Renewed	01/15/2002	08/06/2034
Edwin I. Hatch Nuclear Plant, Unit 2	Georgia	06/13/1978	Renewed	01/15/2002	06/13/2038
Fermi, Unit 2	Michigan	07/15/1985	Application Expected	N/A	03/20/2025
Fort Calhoun Station, Unit 1	Nebraska	08/09/1973	Renewed	11/04/2003	08/09/2033
Grand Gulf Nuclear Station, Unit 1	Mississippi	11/01/1984	Under Review	N/A	11/01/2024
H. B. Robinson Steam Electric Plant, Unit 2	South Carolina	07/31/1970	Renewed	04/19/2004	07/31/2030
Hope Creek Generating Station, Unit 1	New Jersey	07/25/1986	Renewed	07/20/2011	04/11/2046
Indian Point Nuclear Generating, Unit 2	New York	09/28/1973	Under Review	N/A	09/28/2013
Indian Point Nuclear Generating, Unit 3	New York	12/12/1975	Under Review	N/A	12/12/2015
James A. FitzPatrick Nuclear Power Plant	New York	10/17/1974	Renewed	09/08/2008	10/17/2034
Joseph M. Farley Nuclear Plant, Unit 1	Alabama	06/25/1977	Renewed	05/12/2005	06/25/2037

Reactor	State	Date initial operating license issued	License renewal status[a]	Date renewed operating license issued	Date current operating license set to expire
Joseph M. Farley Nuclear Plant, Unit 2	Alabama	03/31/1981	Renewed	05/12/2005	03/31/2041
LaSalle County Station, Unit 1	Illinois	04/17/1982	Application Expected	N/A	04/17/2022
LaSalle County Station, Unit 2	Illinois	12/16/1983	Application Expected	N/A	12/16/2023
Limerick Generating Station, Unit 1	Pennsylvania	08/08/1985	Under Review	N/A	10/26/2024
Limerick Generating Station, Unit 2	Pennsylvania	08/25/1989	Under Review	N/A	06/22/2029
McGuire Nuclear Station, Unit 1	North Carolina	07/08/1981	Renewed	12/05/2003	06/12/2041
McGuire Nuclear Station, Unit 2	North Carolina	05/27/1983	Renewed	12/05/2003	03/03/2043
Millstone Power Station, Unit 2	Connecticut	09/26/1975	Renewed	11/28/2005	07/31/2035
Millstone Power Station, Unit 3	Connecticut	01/31/1986	Renewed	11/28/2005	11/25/2045
Monticello Nuclear Generating Plant, Unit 1	Minnesota	01/09/1981	Renewed	11/08/2006	09/08/2030
Nine Mile Point Nuclear Station, Unit 1	New York	12/26/1974	Renewed	10/31/2006	08/22/2029
Nine Mile Point Nuclear Station, Unit 2	New York	07/02/1987	Renewed	10/31/2006	10/31/2046
North Anna Power Station, Unit 1	Virginia	04/01/1978	Renewed	03/20/2003	04/01/2038
North Anna Power Station, Unit 2	Virginia	08/21/1980	Renewed	03/20/2003	08/21/2040
Oconee Nuclear Station, Unit 1	South Carolina	02/06/1973	Renewed	05/23/2000	02/06/2033
Oconee Nuclear Station, Unit 2	South Carolina	10/06/1973	Renewed	05/23/2000	10/06/2033
Oconee Nuclear Station, Unit 3	South Carolina	07/19/1974	Renewed	05/23/2000	07/19/2034
Oyster Creek Nuclear Generating Station, Unit 1	New Jersey	07/02/1991	Renewed	04/08/2009	04/09/2029
Palisades Nuclear Plant	Michigan	02/24/1971	Renewed	01/17/2007	03/24/2031
Palo Verde Nuclear Generating Station, Unit 1	Arizona	06/01/1985	Renewed	04/21/2011	12/31/2044

Reactor	State	Date initial operating license issued	License renewal status[a]	Date renewed operating license issued	Date current operating license set to expire
Palo Verde Nuclear Generating Station, Unit 2	Arizona	04/24/1986	Renewed	04/21/2011	04/24/2046
Palo Verde Nuclear Generating Station, Unit 3	Arizona	11/25/1987	Renewed	04/21/2011	11/25/2047
Peach Bottom Atomic Power Station, Unit 2	Pennsylvania	10/25/1973	Renewed	05/07/2003	08/08/2033
Peach Bottom Atomic Power Station, Unit 3	Pennsylvania	07/02/1974	Renewed	05/07/2003	07/02/2034
Perry Nuclear Power Plant, Unit 1	Ohio	11/13/1986	Application Expected	N/A	03/18/2026
Pilgrim Nuclear Power Station	Massachusetts	06/08/1972	Renewed	05/29/2012	06/08/2032
Point Beach Nuclear Plant, Unit 1	Wisconsin	10/05/1970	Renewed	12/22/2005	10/05/2030
Point Beach Nuclear Plant, Unit 2	Wisconsin	03/08/1973	Renewed	12/22/2005	03/08/2033
Prairie Island Nuclear Generating Plant, Unit 1	Minnesota	04/05/1974	Renewed	06/27/2011	08/09/2033
Prairie Island Nuclear Generating Plant, Unit 2	Minnesota	10/29/1974	Renewed	06/27/2011	10/29/2034
Quad Cities Nuclear Power Station, Unit 1	Illinois	12/14/1972	Renewed	10/28/2004	12/14/2032
Quad Cities Nuclear Power Station, Unit 2	Illinois	12/14/1972	Renewed	10/28/2004	12/14/2032
River Bend Station, Unit 1	Louisiana	11/20/1985	Application Expected	N/A	08/29/2025
R.E. Ginna Nuclear Power Plant	New York	09/19/1969	Renewed	05/19/2004	09/18/2029
St. Lucie Plant, Unit 1	Florida	03/01/1976	Renewed	10/02/2003	03/01/2036
St. Lucie Plant, Unit 2	Florida	06/10/1983	Renewed	10/02/2003	04/06/2043
Salem Nuclear Generating Station, Unit 1	New Jersey	12/01/1976	Renewed	06/30/2011	08/13/2036
Salem Nuclear Generating Station, Unit 2	New Jersey	05/20/1981	Renewed	06/30/2011	04/18/2040
San Onofre Nuclear Generating Station, Unit 2	California	02/16/1982	Application Expected	N/A	02/16/2022

Reactor	State	Date initial operating license issued	License renewal status[a]	Date renewed operating license issued	Date current operating license set to expire
San Onofre Nuclear Generating Station, Unit 3	California	11/15/1982	Application Expected	N/A	11/15/2022
Seabrook Station, Unit 1	New Hampshire	03/15/1990	Under Review	N/A	03/15/2030
Sequoyah Nuclear Plant, Unit 1	Tennessee	09/17/1980	Under Review	N/A	09/17/2020
Sequoyah Nuclear Plant, Unit 2	Tennessee	09/15/1981	Under Review	N/A	09/15/2021
Shearon Harris Nuclear Power Plant, Unit 1	North Carolina	10/24/1986	Renewed	12/17/2008	10/24/2046
South Texas Project, Unit 1	Texas	03/22/1988	Under Review	N/A	08/20/2027
South Texas Project, Unit 2	Texas	03/28/1989	Under Review	N/A	12/15/2028
Surry Nuclear Power Station, Unit 1	Virginia	05/25/1972	Renewed	03/20/2003	05/25/2032
Surry Nuclear Power Station, Unit 2	Virginia	01/29/1973	Renewed	03/20/2003	01/29/2033
Susquehanna Steam Electric Station, Unit 1	Pennsylvania	07/17/1982	Renewed	11/24/2009	07/17/2042
Susquehanna Steam Electric Station, Unit 2	Pennsylvania	03/23/1984	Renewed	11/24/2009	03/23/2044
Three Mile Island Nuclear Station, Unit 1	Pennsylvania	04/19/1974	Renewed	10/22/2009	04/19/2034
Turkey Point Nuclear Generating, Unit 3	Florida	07/19/1972	Renewed	06/06/2002	07/19/2032
Turkey Point Nuclear Generating, Unit 4	Florida	04/10/1973	Renewed	06/06/2002	04/10/2033
Vermont Yankee Nuclear Power Plant, Unit 1	Vermont	03/21/1972	Renewed	03/21/2011	03/21/2032
Virgil C. Summer Nuclear Station, Unit 1	South Carolina	11/12/1982	Renewed	04/23/2004	08/06/2042
Vogtle Electric Generating Plant, Unit 1	Georgia	03/16/1987	Renewed	06/03/2009	01/16/2047
Vogtle Electric Generating Plant, Unit 2	Georgia	03/31/1989	Renewed	06/03/2009	02/09/2049
Waterford Steam Electric Station, Unit 3	Louisiana	03/16/1985	Application Expected	N/A	12/18/2024
Watts Bar Nuclear Plant, Unit 1	Tennessee	02/07/1996	Intent Not Announced	N/A	11/09/2035

Reactor	State	Date initial operating license issued	License renewal status[a]	Date renewed operating license issued	Date current operating license set to expire
Wolf Creek Generating Station, Unit 1	Kansas	06/04/1985	Renewed	11/20/2008	03/11/2045

Source: NRC.

Note: This appendix lists the 102 commercial nuclear power reactors that were operating in the United States as of May 2013. In February 2013, the owner of the Crystal River Nuclear Plant in Florida permanently shut down that site's reactor and, in May 2013, the owner of the Kewaunee Power Station in Wisconsin permanently shut down that site's reactor. These actions reduced the number of operating commercial nuclear power reactors in the United States from 104 to 102. The Kewaunee reactor was one of the 73 reactors with an operating license renewed by NRC.

[a]"Application Expected" means the owner of the reactor has communicated to NRC its intent to file a license renewal application in the future. "Intent Not Announced" means the owner of the reactor has not communicated to NRC whether or not it intends to file a license renewal application in the future. "Renewed" means NRC has renewed the reactor's operating license. "Under Review" means the owner of the reactor has filed a license renewal application, and NRC is reviewing the application.

Figure 3: Reactors from NRC Region I Included in GAO Review

Millstone Power Station, Unit 3

Source: Dominion Energy.

The Millstone Power Station is located in Waterford, New London County, Connecticut. It is currently operated by Dominion Nuclear Connecticut, Inc.

According to 2010 Census data, Waterford has a population of 19,517. The town's population has remained relatively static over the past 10 years, having increased in size by 365 people, or about 2 percent, since 2000. According to data provided to NRC by reactor owners, in the last quarter of 2012, the 10-mile emergency planning zone population for Millstone Power Station is 124,778, based on 2010 Census data.

Construction permit: Issued – 08/09/1974

Operating license: Issued – 01/31/1986

Renewal application: Submitted – 01/20/2004

Renewed license: Issued – 11/28/2005

Extended operation: Begins – 11/25/2025

License expires: 11/25/2045

Reactor type: Pressurized Water Reactor

Licensed MWt: 3,650

Pilgrim Nuclear Power Station

Source: Courtesy © Entergy Nuclear—Pilgrim Nuclear Power Station.

The Pilgrim Nuclear Power Station is located in Plymouth, Plymouth County, Massachusetts. It is currently operated by Entergy Nuclear Operations, Inc.

According to 2010 Census data, Plymouth's population is 56,468. The town's population has increased slightly over the past 10 years, having increased in size by 4,767 people, or about 9 percent, since 2000. According to data provided to NRC by reactor owners, in the last quarter of 2012, the 10-mile emergency planning zone population for Pilgrim Nuclear Power Station is 93,964, based on 2010 Census data.

Construction permit: Issued – 08/26/1968

Operating license: Issued – 06/08/1972

Renewal application: Submitted – 01/27/2006

Renewed license: Issued – 05/29/2012

Extended operation: Began – 06/08/2012

License expires: 06/08/2032

Reactor type: Boiling Water Reactor

Licensed MWt: 2,028

Figure 4: Reactors from NRC Region II Included in GAO Review

Shearon Harris Nuclear Power Plant, Unit 1

Source: Shearon Harris Nuclear Power Plant, Unit 1.

The Shearon Harris Nuclear Power Plant is located in New Hill, Wake County, North Carolina. It is currently operated by Carolina Power & Light Company.

According to 2010 Census data, the population of New Hill is approximately 1,938. According to data provided to NRC by reactor owners, in the last quarter of 2012, the 10-mile emergency planning zone population for Shearon Harris Nuclear Power Plant is 102,961, based on 2010 Census data.

Construction permit: Issued – 01/27/1978

Operating license: Issued – 10/24/1986

Renewal application: Submitted – 11/14/2006

Renewed license: Issued – 12/17/2008

Extended operation: Begins – 10/24/2026

License expires: 10/24/2046

Reactor type: Pressurized Water Reactor

Licensed MWt: 2,948

Virgil C. Summer Nuclear Station, Unit 1

Source: Virgil C. Summer Nuclear Station, Unit 1.

The Virgil C. Summer Nuclear Station is located in Jenkinsville, Fairfield County, South Carolina. It is currently operated by South Carolina Electric & Gas Company.

Jenkinsville became an incorporated town in 2008, and according to 2010 Census data, the town has a population of 46. According to data provided to NRC by reactor owners, in the last quarter of 2012, the 10-mile emergency planning zone population for Virgil C. Summer Nuclear Station is 12,988, based on 2010 Census data.

Construction permit: Issued – 03/21/1973

Operating license: Issued – 11/12/1982

Renewal application: Submitted – 08/06/2002

Renewed license: Issued – 04/23/2004

Extended operation: Begins – 08/06/2022

License expires: 08/06/2042

Reactor type: Pressurized Water Reactor

Licensed MWt: 2,900

Figure 5: Reactors from NRC Region III Included in GAO Review

Monticello Nuclear Generating Plant, Unit 1

Source: Monticello Nuclear Generating Plant, Unit 1.

The Monticello Nuclear Generating Plant is located in Monticello, Wright County, Minnesota. It is currently operated by Northern States Power Company.

According to 2010 Census data, the population of Monticello is 12,759. The city's population has increased over the past 10 years, having increased in size by 4,891 people, or about 62 percent, since 2000. According to data provided to NRC by reactor owners, in the last quarter of 2012, the 10-mile emergency planning zone population for Monticello Nuclear Generating Plant is 68,635, based on 2010 Census data.

Construction permit: Issued – 06/19/1967

Operating license: Issued – 01/09/1981[a]

Renewal application: Submitted – 03/16/2005

Renewed license: Issued – 11/08/2006

Extended operation: Began – 09/08/2010

License expires: 09/08/2030

Reactor type: Boiling Water Reactor

Licensed MWt: 1,775

Duane Arnold Energy Center

Source: NextEra Energy Duane Arnold.

The Duane Arnold Energy Center is located in Palo, Linn County, Iowa. It is currently operated by NextEra Energy Duane Arnold, LLC.

According to 2010 Census data, the population of Palo is 1,026. The town's population has increased over the past 10 years, having increased in size by 412 people, or about 67 percent, since 2000. According to data provided to NRC by reactor owners, in the last quarter of 2012, the 10-mile emergency planning zone population for Duane Arnold Energy Center is 189,436, based on 2010 Census data.

Construction permit: Issued – 06/22/1970

Operating license: Issued – 02/22/1974

Renewal application: Submitted – 10/01/2008

Renewed license: Issued – 12/16/2010

Extended operation: Begins – 02/21/2014

License expires: 02/21/2034

Reactor type: Boiling Water Reactor

Licensed MWt: 1,912

[a] The Atomic Energy Commission issued a provisional operating license on September 8, 1970, allowing commercial operation. The NRC issued a full-term operating license on January 9, 1981.

Figure 6: Reactors from NRC Region IV Included in GAO Review

Columbia Generating Station	Wolf Creek Generating Station, Unit 1

Source: Columbia Generating Station.

Source: NRC.

The Columbia Generating Station is located in Richland, Benton County, Washington. It is currently operated by Energy Northwest.

According to 2010 Census data, the population of Richland is 48,058. The city's population has increased over the past 10 years, having increased in size by 9,350 people, or about 24 percent, since 2000. According to data provided to NRC by reactor owners, in the last quarter of 2012, the 10-mile emergency planning zone population for Columbia Generating Station is 4,688, based on 2010 Census data.

Construction permit: Issued – 03/19/1973

Operating license: Issued – 04/13/1984

Renewal application: Submitted – 01/20/2010

Renewed license: Issued – 05/22/2012

Extended operation: Begins – 12/20/2023

License expires: 12/20/2043

Reactor type: Boiling Water Reactor

Licensed MWt: 3,486

The Wolf Creek Generating Station is located in Burlington, Coffey County, Kansas. It is currently operated by Wolf Creek Nuclear Operating Corporation.

According to 2010 Census data, the population of Burlington is 2,674. The city's population has decreased slightly over the past 10 years, having decreased in size by 116 people, or about 4 percent, since 2000. According to data provided to NRC by reactor owners, in the last quarter of 2012, the 10-mile emergency planning zone population for Wolf Creek Generating Station is 6,196, based on 2010 Census data.

Construction permit: Issued – 05/31/1977

Operating license: Issued – 06/04/1985

Renewal application: Submitted – 09/27/2006

Renewed license: Issued – 11/20/2008

Extended operation: Begins – 03/11/2025

License expires: 03/11/2045

Reactor type: Pressurized Water Reactor

Licensed MWt: 3,565

Appendix IV: Comments from the Nuclear Regulatory Commission

UNITED STATES
NUCLEAR REGULATORY COMMISSION
WASHINGTON, D.C. 20555-0001

May 10, 2013

Mr. Frank Rusco, Director
Natural Resources and Environment
U.S. Government Accountability Office
441 G Street, NW
Washington, D.C. 20548

Dear Mr. Rusco:

Thank you for providing the U.S. Nuclear Regulatory Commission (NRC) with the opportunity to review and comment on the U.S. Government Accountability Office's (GAO's) draft report GAO-13-493, "Nuclear Reactor License Renewal: NRC Generally Follows Documented Procedures, but Its Revisions to Environmental Review Guidance Have Not Been Timely." The NRC has reviewed the draft report, and has a few minor comments for GAO consideration. Please see the comments in the enclosure to this letter.

If you have any questions regarding the NRC's response, please contact Jesse Arildsen by phone at (301) 415-1785 or by email at Jesse.Arildsen@nrc.gov.

Sincerely,

R. W. Borchardt
Executive Director
for Operations

Enclosure:
As stated

Appendix V: GAO Contact and Staff Acknowledgments

GAO Contact	Frank Rusco, (202) 512-3841 or ruscof@gao.gov
Staff Acknowledgments	In addition to the individual named above, other key contributors to this report were Kimberly Gianopoulos, Assistant Director; David Marroni; Andrew Moore; Kevin Remondini; and Mark Sharoff. Important contributions were also made by Elizabeth Beardsley, Marcia Crosse, John Delicath, Karen Doran, R. Scott Fletcher, Cindy Gilbert, Jonathan Kucskar, David Maurer, and Kiki Theodoropoulos.